TAKING A BITE OUT
OF FOOD WASTE

TAKING A BITE OUT OF FOOD WASTE

A CLOSER LOOK AT WHAT WE'RE LEAVING ON THE TABLE

ADRIAN HERTEL

NEW DEGREE PRESS

TAKING A BITE OUT OF FOOD WASTE

A Closer Look at What We're Leaving on the Table

ISBN   978-1-64137-040-0   *Paperback*

ISBN   978-1-64137-041-7   *Ebook*

CONTENTS

INTRODUCTION

———

BACK TO THE ROOTS

The pot in front of me was filled with the spaghetti noodles and tomato sauce I'd just cooked. As a proud member of an Italian family, this scene was not unusual, save the part about my mother yelling at me. (Okay, in fairness, that happens on occasion as well.)

"Why are you eating out of the *same pot* you cooked these in?" she questioned loudly.

I hadn't really thought about it. My process had been to warm up the sauce in a pan and, when the sauce was ready and the noodles had reached al-dente perfection, I would simply drain the noodles and dump them *directly* into the pan of fragrant tomato sauce. Then I'd grabbed the pan with my meal by the handle, walked to the table and sat down to eat, with a peaceful look of satisfaction on my face.

And yet my mother found a way of interrupting my 'pasta zen' moment.

"You're just like my mom's dad," she said with a laugh.

"What do you mean?"

"He would eat straight out of the pot, just as you are doing!"

"Well it's one less plate to wash," I replied. I smiled, proud of my idea, but mostly happy about my meal.

My mother decided to take this as her cue to *re*-remind me of our family history (stories I'd heard dozens of times growing up). But this story was unique—and would be one that I couldn't quite shake after hearing it. Referring to her maternal grandparents—frugal immigrants from poverty-stricken southern Italy—she began to share a story I'd never heard before:

"My grandma and grandpa, your great-grandparents, used to cook all of their meals with just enough ingredients for two and mostly in one pot. To save the water necessary for clean up, when the meal was ready, my grandpa would stand over the sink and eat out of the pot and, when he was done, he would pass the spoon and the pot onto my grandma, who would eat the rest."

She paused as if reflecting on the details she'd seen time after time growing up, before she continued with a few more anecdotes. In the end, she summarized it all with one sentence.

"And, nothing, and I do mean nothing, was left behind; nothing would be thrown out."

By the time she was done with her story, I was done with my meal. I smiled looking down at my empty pot and thought to myself, "Hmmm, just like them...not bad."

But the core similarity between my great-grandparents' eating habits and mine did not strike me as significant at the time; I realize now, however, that it was one of the first clues into my family's history of fighting food waste—a fight that, as will be explained in this book, is of critical importance around the world, but especially here in America.

LEADERS OF THE PACK

While America plays a prime role in many areas we can boast about, it also plays a leading role in areas that make us less proud, namely in that of food waste. In fact, Americans throw away a whopping 40% of all food at some point throughout the supply chain.

Despite my ability to have my pots double as dinner ware—introducing "one-pot meals" to my eating habits in the truest sense of the term—my family and I probably contributed our fair share to those stats. We would eat what we wanted on our plates and scrape the remainder into the trash can or garbage disposal. When we'd cook, we'd throw away foods that were partially brown or ugly. We would regularly load up at the grocery store and when we'd come back from our shopping sprees, we'd toss out all the "old," "expired" (or "nearly expired') foods and replace them with a new batch, without batting an eyelash.

Honestly, I figured it was just par for the course.

And as an American, it probably is. Perhaps because we are affluent and food prices are relatively cheap, perhaps because food is plentiful or perhaps because of our habits, preferences, and our penchant for convenience, the spoilage continues. Interestingly, however, according to a study from the National Resources Defense Council (NRDC), most people think they have nothing to do with the problem. The NRDC found that 76% of people believe they throw out less food than the average American. Yet 90% of Americans throw out food too soon, according to the NRDC. The numbers just don't add up.

The facts speak for themselves and the consequences affect us in many ways, ranging from important economic and social issues to lasting and detrimental environmental problems as well.

According to a study published in the Public Library of Science, the amount of food Americans waste has increased over 50% in the last four decades.[1] Dick Peixoto, owner and grower of Lakeside Organic Gardens put this into perspective when he said:

"What we throw away in California [farms] for cosmetic reasons could end world hunger."

While this is an exaggeration, it's not too far from the truth. If just one-fourth of the food currently lost or wasted globally could be saved, it would be enough to feed the 870 million hungry people in the world.[2]

MORE THAN A PILE OF BEANS

Over the course of the next months, I started to think about my own behavior more and more and even started to research the problem. But I really didn't get much further than that.

It's not *my* problem, I often rationalized. At least *I* was becoming educated on the issue, right?

But one fall day changed all that and made me decide it actually *was* my problem. That was the day I was fortunate enough to be seated next to Lynette Johnson, Executive Director of the Society of St. Andrews (SoSA); SoSA is a faith-based nonprofit organization dedicated, among other things, to reducing food loss and feeding the hungry.

As a part of my light fascination with food waste, I'd periodically note local events about the subject. One day an announcement for the *2nd Annual National Food Recovery Dialogue*, held by the Food Recovery Network, hit my radar. As luck would have it, it was being held in in Washington, D.C., which meant I could be there in less than 20 minutes.

Johnson, who also attended the event, introduced me to SoSA and the organization's contribution to solving one small piece of the food waste problem—the 1.1 billion pounds of food SoSA estimates is lost *just* on U.S. farms every year. Keep in mind that this doesn't include the billions wasted as the food is transported, packaged, displayed for sale and ultimately purchased and used (or not) by end-consumers in kitchens and restaurants.

"See these beans," she said, showing me the photo below. The beans originate from one singular farm. "The farmer's contract was for green beans between three to five inches in length." She paused briefly. "All the others would be thrown away, including that truckload." She spoke as she pointed to the picture of the contents of a fully loaded truck.

Johnson's organization helped to recover these "out of spec but perfectly good" foods. But this pile was representative of just one farm in one small region in which she operated. "This load is just one small part of the overall problem," she said, matter of factly. After all, this picture was reality to her—a reality that had lost its shock value.

But for me, it prompted a very different reaction. It brought my mind back to the story from my mother and her parents.

"You're just like my mom's dad," she had said.

And yet here I was, nothing like them. I didn't think about wasting. I had no idea how much food waste was happening around me and I'd done very little to even make a dent in it.

This was the moment I would actually start to take action. But how?

'BREAKING BAD' HABITS

I spent the next several days consuming more information about food waste and how I could make my contribution to reducing the problem. The biggest thing I realized was that if I planned to make actual changes in my life—not just thinking or reading or doing one thing—but making these changes a habit, I'd need more than just a well-intentioned shock from a pile of beans that were to be thrown away.

I needed a system.

Enter Charles Duhigg.

Charles would be my Sherpa, or at least one of them, guiding me in how to make this desire into a habit. And fortunately for me, he was the expert. Charles had quite literally written the book on The Power of Habits.

As Duhigg told author Daniel Pink in an interview:

> Scientists have explained that every habit is made up of a cue, a routine and a reward. The cue is a trigger that tells your brain to go into automatic mode and which habit to use. Then there is the routine—the behavior itself—which can be physical or mental or emotional. Finally, there is a reward, which helps your brain figure out if this particular habit is worth remembering for the future. Over time, this loop—cue, routine, reward; cue, routine, reward—becomes more automatic as the cue and reward become neurologically intertwined.

> Take exercise. Studies have shown that people who identify simple cues and clear rewards are more likely to establish consistent exercise habits. If you want to start running in the morning, for instance, research indicates you're more likely to succeed if you choose an obvious cue (like always putting on your sneakers before breakfast or leaving your running clothes next to your bed) and a clear reward (like a treat afterwards or the sense of accomplishment that comes from recording your miles in a log book). After a while, your brain will start anticipating that reward—craving the treat or the feeling of accomplishment—and there will be a measurable neurological impulse to exercise each day.

If I was to truly make a change in my life—and potentially help others do the same—I needed to figure out how to make a habit out of reducing food waste. I needed to create my own set of cues, routines and rewards, and something others could use too.

Committing to finding a new routine did not come easily. I spent a lot of time thinking about my behavior and one day was unexpectedly jolted into action by a summer experience—two diametrically opposed ones to be exact—and the additional insight I got from Justin Brewer and other experts in habits.

This book details my own quest to change my behavior to save more food and research the subject matter more deeply. Along the way, my similarities to my great-grandparents and grandparents became more and more vivid. In fact, by writing this book and making changes in my life, I realized that I had tapped into my forgotten heritage of fighting food waste. I also realized that we can all make a difference, and there is plenty of opportunity for those who do.

MY FOOD WASTE JOURNEY

This book is a collection of facts, stories, anecdotes and approaches used to develop my own habitual approach to reducing food waste. Inside the book you'll also learn:

- The role war played and continued to play in food conservation efforts;
- How my certification as an official Neapolitan Pizza-Maker, followed by a 'WWOOFer' experience turned me into a literal food waste fanatic;
- Why the EPA is a hidden champion of food waste and what a local grab-and-go grocery taught me about the problem that surprised me;
- How established business can and are contributing to reducing food waste;
- About five startups that are tackling the problem including one all the way in Japan and one started by a classmate of mine;
- And more about the *Curious Case of Green Bean Drops* that ultimately was the *cue* to kickstart my own journey.

Once again, my journey didn't necessarily come easily, but it's a system I've learned and one that others can easily implement in their own way. And it's something I've even gotten my skeptical mother to embrace (more on that later).

EVERY LITTLE BIT(E) COUNTS

In my journey to understand the food waste problem, I turned to my past. I performed countless interviews with friends and family, only to discover that, for me, the 'Food Waste Prevention Die' was already cast and had landed on

'Hooked'. I happened to be part of a lineage of people who took food waste seriously and did something about it. Some members of my family, like others today, even earned money addressing the problem!

After having one of the most wasteful personal experiences of my life—learning to make pizza and working in a restaurant—I went back to my roots and to a much simpler life, a life on the farm. With little to sustain me, other than what the earth provided, I learned to make the most of it. I also learned that with a little bit of effort, there was surprisingly plenty to be had. My inherited and developed abilities to reduce our food waste problem set me on my journey, and confirmed that we all have a part to play in addressing the issue, including the government, corporations, fancy startups or a lowly college student like yours truly. You just have to care.

THE POT-O'-GOLD AT THE END OF THE RAINBOW

And, when it comes to food waste, those who do care are rewarded emotionally, morally and financially. In addition to individuals, many corporations have also embraced sustainability issues, including those related to food waste, thus improving image, company morale and the bottom line. Publications are writing intriguing stories about food waste every day. Governments are also increasingly playing their part to address the food waste problem. New start-ups, both for-profit and not-for-profit, see plenty of opportunity in this space, as do I. In this book you'll learn about many of these efforts as well as tips for reducing food waste as an individual.

Returning to the problem, we have to ask ourselves: Are current efforts enough to save 40% of perfectly good food going un-eaten in America?

Not quite.

But we can look to other countries for guidance. Denmark for example, has slashed its food waste by 25% in just 5 years![3] This is largely thanks to one woman, Selina Juul, and the lobby group she founded, Stop Wasting Food (Stop Spild Af Mad).

Successes like that of Denmark combined with the ever-increasing awareness of the food waste problem in the United States make me very hopeful that we are on the path to solving this problem. The first step to fixing the food waste problem is recognizing that it is fixable.

PART 1

UNDERSTANDING THE FOOD WASTE PROBLEM

CHAPTER 1

FACT AND ISSUES

———

People are starving not because we don't have enough food,
but because we're not organized around solving that problem.

—LARRY PAGE, CO-FOUNDER, GOOGLE

Food waste is a nexus issue. It involves money, it involves people, and it involves the environment. It also involves taking the time to gain a broader understanding of the facts and figures, how waste happens and why. It touches on so many areas that everyone has a reason to rally behind the cause and become a Food Waste Warrior (more on this in Part 3) in their own right.

THE FACTS & ISSUES

Lets start with a few basic facts:

- Roughly 40% of food in America is wasted every year[1] (30% on a worldwide basis)[2]. It's almost like buying two big grocery bags and dropping one while walking back to your car, getting in, and driving away. "No one would do that," you'd say, and you'd be right—consumers only waste 25% percent of what they buy[1]—but the system we all support with our hard-earned money does the rest.
- 50% of vegetables and seafood are never eaten.[3]
- 90% of us throw away food too soon. Part of it is our fault for having overly high standards and another part is due to the unregulated and confusing food expiration date labeling, which causes us to believe perfectly good food is unsafe to eat (more on this later).[1]
- A family of four throws out up to $2275 of food a year. Name me one family who can't think of something better to do with that cash than throw in the garbage and I'll eat their trash![1]
- America spends $218 billion growing and processing food that is never eaten—**that's 1.3% of the GDP.**[4]
- Each one of us tosses out over 300lbs of food a year. That's a pretty big garbage bag by any standard.[1]
- Developed countries (such as Europe and US) waste significantly more at the consumer level than other developing countries. The abundance and wealth prevalent in Western societies leads us to waste more.[5]

- 95% of the food we throw away ends up in landfills or combustion facilities And, on the flip side, only 5% of food scraps get composted.[6]
- Uneaten food at 21% is the largest proportion of our total landfill volume; it takes up 18% of our total arable land and uses 25% of our country's fresh water supply.[6]
- 41.2 million Americans struggle to put food on the table.[7]
- 40% of American-grown produce is never consumed.[1]

AND

- 38 million tons of food is wasted in America each year.[6] That's 50% more than in 1990 and 300% more than what Americans discarded in 1960.[8]
- If just one-fourth of the food currently lost or wasted globally could be saved, it would be enough to feed the 870 million hungry people in the world.[2]

THE IMPACTS

As mentioned and alluded to in the above points, the negative impacts of wasting food can be generally categorized into three areas: economic, environmental and social.

ECONOMIC:

In addition to some of the figures set out above, it is estimated that, at the retail and consumer levels in the United States, food loss and waste totals $161 billion dollars a year. According to a June 2017 article from the Huffington Post, "[r]ight now the resulting economic loss is somewhere between 780 billion and 1 trillion dollars a year."[9] Food waste occurs both on a private and on a commercial level and therefore carries a big price tag—remember the GDP figure above. In addition, producing food that is thrown out wastes money, time and resources. In short, our food waste habits make zero economic sense.

ENVIRONMENTAL:

Food waste also poses major problems for our environment. Food constitutes the single largest stream of materials placed into American trash—some 38 million tons each year, according to the Environmental Protection Agency (EPA).[6] Only a scant 5% of organic materials is diverted for reuse.[6] The rest occupies landfills, where it decomposes, and produces methane, a powerful greenhouse gas, which is 23 times more harmful to the environment than carbon dioxide. Global food waste adds 3.3 billion tons of greenhouse gases to the planet's atmosphere annually.[5]

Yet, when we picture the stuff that's hurting our planet, what *do* we think of? We think of smoke stacks, we think of cars, and we think of oil spills. We don't really think about all the food we throw away: roughly 200 million pounds of it every day! (based on 38 million tons annually[6] / 365 days) In fact, if it were a country, the land devoted to growing wasted food globally would be the second largest country in the world and, according to the Food & Agriculture Organization of the United Nations, it would be the third largest emitter of greenhouse gases. That's not a ribbon anyone should want to wear. So suffice it to say that our food waste habits are killing our planet.

SOCIAL:

From a societal point of view, our food waste habits are not only senseless but also shameful. In 2016, 41.2 million people were living in food-insecure households at some time during the year, simply not knowing where their next meal was coming from.[7] Yet, we think it is perfectly acceptable to waste green beans that are not 'just right'. According to the Huffington Post article referenced above, "...with approximately the same amount of money [wasted globally], or less, all of the [...] people who are going hungry every day, could be fed." Let me repeat: *all* of them. So, it is fair to say that, in a world where 870 million go hungry every year, our food waste habits are really, really wasteful.[2]

FOOD WASTE'S RELATIONSHIP WITH HUNGER

Let's take a closer look at food waste's relationship to hunger, particularly as it affects the United States. As stated above, roughly 41.2 million people, one in eight households, lived in food-insecure households in 2016, regularly unable to get nutritious food.[7] This occurs while millions of pounds of food are being thrown away every day. Dr. Roni Neff, a Johns Hopkins University researcher, led the first ever study examining the nutrients Americans are tossing into the garbage and found that 'We could provide a 2000 calorie diet to 84% of the population.'" In other words, our waste contains important nutrients, such as dietary fiber, Vitamin C and calcium, that so many are sorely lacking and that would help them lead healthier lives.

In addition to what we are throwing in the trash, as we saw from the picture of beans, many more millions of pounds of food are simply left unharvested to rot in fields. The efforts of SoSA, mentioned above, are welcome in this regard. Unfortunately, they are not easily scalable so they merely make a dent in the problem. Nonprofit commercial operations similar to SoSA also exist and are making an impact. (See Adrian's Top 5 in Part 3) But at the end of the day, more has to happen. Tristram Stuart alluded to this "more" in an interview for the recently released food waste documentary, "Wasted! The Story of Food Waste". Stuart is practically the face of the food waste movement, having working on the issue since 2009 as an author, activist, founder of Feedback 5000 and winner of international environmental Sophie Prize. This is what he had to say:

Everyone cares about hunger. There is a tremendous need. The issue isn't a lack of food for those who are starving, it's a distribution problem. But it goes deeper than this.

In my view, the deeper thing or the 'more' that has to happen is that we have to change our poor food waste habits.

Changing bad habits is not easy, as I'm sure you will agree. It is even harder if you don't even know you have them. If you don't even think you're part of the problem, how will you improve?

IT'S NOT ME, IT'S HIM

Yes that's right, interestingly enough, almost no one—including me a few months back—feels responsible for the food waste problem. The NRDC found this out in a survey, which determined that most people think they aren't part of the problem. 70% believe changing behavior would reduce food waste in their home little or not at all.

One of the reasons we don't feel we are part of the problem might be because we simply don't see the food we waste. It disappears so quickly. We barely even notice our half-eaten plates being whisked away at a restaurant because we are enjoying our conversation too much. A magical conveyor belt at the college dining hall just carries our waste away to a magical land where it evaporates into thin air, right? We throw things away habitually and unconsciously (look out for my onion story in the next part), so the waste simply seems not to happen. Or, the waste happens before it ever reaches us, like piles of fruits and vegetables left on the ground to rot because they are 'imperfect' or 'ugly'. Later I will introduce you to fields of cauliflower left unharvested because sun exposure turned them yellow—they got a sun tan—but for now just remember the green beans in the parking lot.

So although surveys reveal that most Americans think that they don't waste food, statistics say they are wrong. Just ask Lillian Leeser, who had a lifelong career in catering. While waste is an issue that plagues the catering industry in general, one of Leeser's employers wasted an inordinate amount of food. "It was too disturbing. It made me sick," she said. Unlike the attendees of the event she was catering, she was forced to bear witness to the waste when she cleaned up at the end of the day. One day she "couldn't bear it any longer." She quit soon after.

What if you saw all the waste you were responsible for? How would you feel then? How would it affect you? What if you saw your plate scraps for the year piled up on a conveyor belt and getting higher and higher? What if you saw the price you paid for these scraps? What if you smelled your food scraps beginning to decompose, grow mold and seep into your carpeted floor and disintegrate it? Or what if you just stopped to take another look at the picture of a parking lot full of beans and ask yourself the question again: "How do I feel about food waste?"

My pizza experience (see Part II) made me do just that, and that's when I realized there is no such thing as 'just throwing it away.' That is when I really started realizing that I am part of the problem and, to varying degrees, that we all are.

CHAPTER 2

UNDERSTANDING FOOD LOSS VS. FOOD WASTE

———

Before we proceed, it is important to understand certain key terminology related to the topic of food waste and particularly one important distinction: the difference between food 'loss' and food 'waste,' where this happens and why.

FOOD LOSS VS. FOOD WASTE

Food 'loss' encompasses the food that, for a host of reasons, does not make it to market. Common causes are that the food is considered irregular or 'ugly,' like the beans in the parking lot.

Or these unharvested potatoes rescued by SoSA. (Putting the 'Drop' in 'Potato Drop').

Or these tomatoes let to rot in Tenerife.

Or this 'sea' of abandoned Valencia oranges in California.

I think you get the point!

Food 'waste', on the other hand, is the term for food that stores, restaurants and consumers accept but then end up tossing, also for a variety of reasons.

DEVELOPED VS DEVELOPING COUNTRIES

The terms "Food loss" and "food waste" together capture the two types of waste that are generated along the food supply chain. Simply, food loss happens at the beginning of the chain and food waste occurs at the end. Food loss is a greater concern in developing countries, accounting for 84% to 95% of the food that goes uneaten there. Half the food produced in developing countries never makes it to market and 630 million tons of food, or $310 billion dollars, is lost every year in developing countries as a result of this waste. The reasons for these significant post-harvest losses include the "financial and structural limitations in harvest techniques, storage and transport infrastructures, combined with climatic conditions favorable to food spoilage." (FAO, Food wastage footprint—Impacts on natural resources) Moreover, small-scale farmers, the largest producers of food in developing countries, are disproportionately disadvantaged by these factors.

Food waste, on the other hand, is a relatively smaller problem in developing countries. Food waste is in many cases a product of wealth, a luxury that developing countries simply cannot afford.

Although—as we saw in the above pictures—food loss does occur in developed countries such as the United States, food *waste* is the bigger problem here as outlined in the 'Facts and Figures' in Chapter 1.

Researchers such as the Food and Agricultural Association of the United Nations (FAO) and the World Food Program have identified opportunities to fight both food loss and food waste all along the supply chain.

As mentioned above with respect to food loss, access to information and education, as well as innovative solutions to transport and energy problems can greatly reduce the problem in developing countries. Similar tactics can be applied in developed nations as well. Fortunately, businesses and private/public partnerships are working to this end, for example offering innovative apps that provide farmers with information on weather conditions, packaging and sensors that keep products fresh longer, or training on sustainable farming practices.

With respect to food waste in developed countries, commercial solutions are sprouting up as well. Just take Copia, a startup that collects leftover food from corporate meetings and delivers it to local charities, offering tax benefits to the corporate donor. (For other commercial solutions, see *Adrian's Top 5 List* in Part III.)

Individuals can also contribute to improving the food waste problem by voluntarily changing certain habits, such as not stuffing their refrigerators to capacity (which makes food go bad more quickly because of the lack of air circulation), not buying in bulk (if they don't have a 'bulk' appetite), and actually eating their leftovers, for example.

One particular food waste reduction strategy that interested me was being 'forced' to change one's behavior or habits. This was the case for diners at the University of California at Santa Barbara (UCSB) cafeteria. Having noticed the large amount of uneaten food left over on trays after meals, administrators eliminated the dining trays so that diners could carry less food to the table at a time. This simple trick forced a behavioral change and markedly reduced the amount of uneaten food left behind by diners, decreasing the dining hall's food waste by 50% (*Food Waste*).

INTERVIEW WITH PAPA—ONE MAN'S FOOD WASTE BEHAVIOR

In an effort to deepen my understanding of individual behavior, I interviewed my father, a man known for reflecting deeply on these matters. I wanted to look closely at one individual's behaviors—both voluntary and involuntary—regarding the topic of food waste (and he happened to be there and interested).

My father grew up in Cologne, Germany. His father fought in World War II, and his mother lived through it. Given that his parents had suffered through war, food waste had no place in his home. In other words, bad food waste habits simply could not be formed; they were not allowed.

My father grew up hearing war stories from his father. My grandfather told him that during the war, he would trade old food bits for other old food bits. He said that eggs were precious and hard to come by. His parents often only had access to those that were cracked—the ones we would all simply toss today—and they would treasure them. Hard and stale bread would be readily consumed. Food was difficult to come by during the war and, even though it was often dull and dreary, anything that could be eaten would be. Soldiers often stopped in fields to pull raw potatoes out of the ground, their stomachs achy and empty. My grandfather kept the habits he was forced into and similarly compelled his family to adopt them even after the war ended. His wife would make jam with old or bruised fruit, tea bags would be reused and whatever was not eaten at lunch made it to the table for dinner. That is how my father grew up; that was his norm.

My papa is not as frugal or extreme as his father, but, as a result of his upbringing, he has not only adopted certain good food saving behaviors but also voluntarily formed a few of his own. For example, not happy about the amount of food waste we were producing as a family when we moved from Germany to America, he was one of the first people to sign up for the composting program in Princeton when it was introduced. He even sent a letter thanking the township for this initiative. He puts compostable waste into the marked bin as if on autopilot and regularly goes through the normal trash to ensure that things that got there by mistake find their rightful home in the compost bin. He doesn't even think about it, it just happens.

And the reward is how good he feels about not having to drag so many heavy, smelly trash bins to the curb, not to mention saving so much food from decomposing in a landfill.

My papa, like many of us, grew up in an urban environment. But he also spent a lot of time working on his family's small farm in the countryside as a kid. These different experiences led him to the following insight, which he shared during our conversation:

> Civilization has detached us from the circle of life. The natural cycle in which an overripe pear drops from the branch onto the ground and enriches many different animals, insects and plants doesn't take place. Instead that circle of life is abruptly cut short the moment that pear lands in our trash can.

He thinks it is important to look back on the 'olden days' when leftover food scraps were fed to the dogs and the pigs. "My family had a summer house out in the country side. All the local farmers gave their leftovers to their animals. There was no waste in those days." My dad's commitment to reduce food waste and put waste that cannot be avoided to good use is his contribution to the cause. Because of his upbringing, he is familiar with the problem of food waste and knows the potential uneaten food holds to benefit rather than harm. Unfortunately, that is not the case for everyone.

CORRECT ANSWER: 25 YEARS!

Take this example: In the movie *Waste! The Story of Food Waste*, a group of young, intelligent-looking 20-somethings were asked how long they thought it took for a head of lettuce to decompose in a landfill. The answers ranged from "a couple of weeks" to "a couple of months". No one guessed the right answer: 25 years! (I asked my father the same question and although he did not hit the nail on the head, his guess was the closest of all.)

The people surveyed in the film did not grow up like my father, cultivating the forced and learned behaviors as my father did. They also did not understand the lifecycle of food, which (slowly) rots in landfills. Most people interviewed in the film were of the view that food simply decomposes, seeps into the soil and fertilizes it. Ta-da! What they didn't know was that food trapped under piles of trash, without oxygen, undergoes anaerobic decomposition. Instead of nutrient-rich, fertile soil, this process creates methane, a strong greenhouse gas that eats away at our ozone layer and contributes to climate change. My father knew all this. I, until recently, did not.

CHAPTER 3

THE CURIOUS CASE OF GREEN BEAN DROPS IN THE NIGHT

———

To truly understand the problem of food waste, it helps to start with a story, and I can think of no better one than *The Curious Case of the Green Bean Drops in the Night.*

For that, you have to go to southern Tennessee—at least mentally. Picture a hot and humid day—normal by all accounts—at the peak of the harvesting season. If you try really hard, you might even be able to hear the hum of farm machinery extracting produce from the fields, as you (mentally) drive down rural country roads.

My virtual excursion was admittedly a bit easier because I attended the *2nd Annual National Food Recovery Dialogue* in Washington D.C., complete with storytellers and pictures on a big screen. One particular picture stuck out in my mind. It was of a farm and the reason it remained so vivid was mainly because of what it produced: bright green beans.

The picture was as telling as it was colorful. At the edge of the property one could see an old, worn-out conveyor belt. It appeared to whir and rattle tirelessly, as it shot a blurry stream of green beans into a tractor-trailer, already almost filled to capacity. The beans were in quite a rush. Why, you ask? Well, green beans have a very short shelf life, so freshly picked beans, like the ones from this Tennessee farm, had places to go and people to see. At least that is what they thought.

"But these beans weren't destined to be eaten," explained Lynette Johnson, interrupting my thoughts. Johnson is the Executive Director of SoSA, who I introduced you to earlier. SoSA is America's oldest and largest gleaning organization.

GLEANING

> The act of collecting leftover crops from farmers' fields after they have been commercially harvested or on fields where it is not economically profitable to harvest.

Back to the beans. Johnson went on to explain, in her cool, collected and nonchalant style, that these particular beans had another destiny. Her intellect and her demeanor left a big impression on me; so did the next words she shared.

"The farmer's contract was for green beans between three to five inches in length." She paused briefly to let the deceptively innocent words sink in.

"All the others would be thrown away, including that truck-load." She spoke as she pointed to a freeze-frame picture of the fully loaded truck.

"Wait, what?" I asked in disbelief. "That's not where I expected this story to go."

Johnson smirked, having predicted my reaction.

"Why don't they sell them?" I continued. "Is there something wrong with them?"

"Nothing is *wrong* with them," she answered very matter-of-factly. "They're perfectly good green beans, but his contract was *exclusive*." She stressed the word in a way she hoped I'd understand, but I didn't so she explained it to me.

The farmer in question, like most other farmers, had a contract with a corporate buyer. This buyer required the farmer to provide a 'standard' product, in this case green beans between three and five inches in length. Not only do these kinds of 'exclusive' agreements state that the buyer will not accept beans that do not fit this definition—the 'imperfect' produce—but also the contracts bar the farmer from selling the 'rejects' to anyone else. As a result, any greens beans that did not meet the arbitrarily set cosmetic standards of the purchaser, in this case a packing house, would have to be dumped into a nearby pit.

"Not even composted! The HORROR!" I thought, as my mind briefly drifted to my dad.

"Why does the farmer not simply donate them then?" I asked naively.

Johnson had an answer for that as well. Given green beans' short shelf life, the US Food and Drug Administration (USFDA) mandates they be removed from the farmer's property within 24 hours of harvest, in order to prevent a food safety risk, or be stored. "That's very expensive," Johnson explained. "Most farmers can't afford it." Johnson went on to tell me that SoSA had helped one of their partner farmers raise the money necessary to implement refrigeration units to store the produce until volunteers could come and pick everything up for further distribution, but they then "realized that these refrigeration units require a lot of time and effort to clean and maintain, which ends up costing the farmer more money he does not have."

And so, with more and more 'irregular' or 'ugly' green beans coming out of the field every hour and with nowhere to store or sell them, this particular farmer was forced to haul them off his land and dump them into a local pit. That was the sad, dark fate for the bright, green beans.

Worse still, this 20,000-pound truckload of 'rejects' was not the first one of the day to be collected, Johnson said. The farmer's machines worked all day long, sorting and combing through fresh-picked beans, and automatically separating out those that didn't meet the length specifications. Those cullings come to 1,000 pounds of green beans every 10 minutes. As a result, every three hours, every day of the harvest season, a new truck was filled. And, if that were not already bad enough, there were five farms on the same road doing the same thing.

If you are like me, you probably find it hard to picture this massive volume of food. You probably also have a hard time understanding how so much fresh, green produce could be headed to the graveyard for no reason other than the fact that it were not 'perfect' according to *somebody's* definition. Johnson leaned over to me as she scrolled through a slide deck, looking for something specific. Something to show me the proportions of what a truckload of beans looks like in real life.

"Look at this one," she said, turning her iPhone screen to me. On the floor of a parking lot sat a veritable mountain of green beans, surrounded on all sides by people in portable chairs.

A picture says it all.

SOURCE: THE SOCIETY OF ST. ANDREWS

This information was all very new and shocking to me, but Johnson seemed a bit bored. She had experienced this situation many times before, so her attention started drifting off to a conversation at a nearby table.

I didn't fault her for this. As executive director of an organization recovering 25+ million pounds of produce annually, this was just another pile and the numbers she cited were just another statistic, just another blip on the radar. She very clearly cared about the issue, but she had also told this story hundreds of times. It had lost its shock value. The 25+ million pounds Johnson's organization recovers is a lot; more than any other gleaning organization in America. However, the recovered food still only represents 2.5% of the 1.1 billion pounds of produce SoSA estimates is wasted on U.S. farms every year.

Modern agriculture has replaced much of the manual labor that is required to get healthy food to our tables. It is one of the reasons the cost of food is so low in the United States. On the flipside, however, these advances in speed, precision and abundance have also allowed purchasers the power of choice, a lot of which they now leave to a machine. But here's what a machine (and the people who program it too, for that matter) doesn't know about green beans: whether too short, or too long or already snapped, beans or produce of any shape or size is still tasty and nutritious.

The Society of St. Andrews regularly organizes 'crop drops' such as the one pictured above. Once it has recovered the produce, it starts looking for dozens of volunteers to help sort 20,000 pounds of unmarketable but totally tasty fruits and vegetables. As a result of SoSA's efforts, a great deal of food has been saved and distributed to people who need it. People who regularly lack access to nutritious food do not judge a bean by its length.

One of the Society Of St. Andrews's keys to success is "its religious foundations," Johnson explained. "Because we are faith-based, it allows us to be rapid-response. Even in a new state, if a farmer rings us up, I can call three churches and have 20 volunteers available in two, three days. No other gleaning organization can do that!" she remarked, visibly proud about this fact.

As mentioned, according to current food safety laws, farmers are required to get all their produce off their property within 24 hours. "With no customer to sell it to, and with more green beans out in the field, without our organization, perfectly good food would simply get hauled off to a local dumping pit or be left to rot in the field." When I asked what the farmer thought of all this she added, "It's the sad truth. For many farmers, these massive and regular volumes of waste are just the 'cost of doing business.'"

At this point in our conversation, the next speaker at the conference was getting ready to start her presentation. The speaker was Joann Berkenkamp, a Senior Advocate of the Food & Agriculture Program, of the National Resources

Defense Council (NRDC). The NRDC is a group of passionate activists, scientists, lawyers and policy advocates working to safeguard the earth. Berkenkamp was at the conference to present the results of a 'first-of-its-kind' study of urban food waste, examining three major metropolitan areas: New York City, Denver, and Nashville. The report was intended to quantify the potential for multiple sectors of the urban food economy to expand food donations. Among other things, the study had included estimated costs of implementing solutions to the problems the research had identified.

"We eventually arrived at this table," Berkenkamp said, pointing to the next slide. "It breaks down the cost of rescuing 50% of all otherwise wasted food from grocery stores, restaurants, events, et cetera, and redistributing it," Berkenkamp explained. When she addressed a particular part of the slide, which listed the estimated cost per pound of food recovery, Johnson scoffed.

"One dollar a pound?!" she spoke under her breath, visibly more roused than before. "We're at 9 cents a pound!" she whispered from the side of her mouth.

At first, I too was shocked by this dramatic difference in price. But then I realized I wasn't comparing apples to apples. First off, the NRDC's report detailed urban food recovery solutions which address the problem of food waste at the end of the supply chain, while SoSA's approach prevents food loss at the beginning of the supply chain. These are inherently different problems that will require different solutions, making the approaches not readily comparable. Second is the scalability of each approach. Before I say what I am going to say next, I want to recognize, commend even, the fantastic work of the thousands of volunteer-based groups and organizations like SoSA fighting hunger, food waste and food loss around the country, organizations that dedicate countless hours to recovering food and helping those who need it. SoSA transformed that truckload of rescued, 'too-short or too-long goodness' pictured above into 60,000 nutritious and delicious servings for hungry people in surrounding counties and states! And, as I just learned, SoSA did it at a fraction of the cost others were able to.

Unfortunately, however commendable they are, SoSA's efforts are, in my opinion, not scalable. No volunteer organization can handle 'Green Bean Drops' every two hours for an entire season at thousands of farms across the nation. It is just not possible.

To demonstrate the infeasibility of a universal volunteer-based solution, let us examine another SoSA 'Crop Drop' from earlier in 2017. Another good story. In the middle of one starry night, a truck dumped 11,450 pounds of green beans in the parking lot of the Bellevue Presbyterian Church in Nashville, Tennessee. This is, by any account, an odd time for a church to be open, but that's when the farmer finished packing the beans that hadn't made the cut. Given the time limit mentioned above, he couldn't wait until morning to haul them off his land. And so, the church drop happened at an 'ungodly' hour—pardon the pun. SoSA had to work all night to pull volunteers together. Fortunately, by the time the sun came up, they had managed to cobble together over 120 boy scouts, community volunteers and church members. Even though the load was only half the size as the one pictured above, they all still had to work from 8 a.m. to noon to bag the entire pile into 8-pound, family-sized bags.

Despite its higher cost, I believe that a well-designed commercial or governmental approach is the better solution to the problems of food waste and food loss. In addition, as we all know thanks to economies of scale, costs go down over time as more food is rescued. In fact, in the aforementioned NRDC report, the cost per pound to recover food fell by almost 40% after a 25% increase in total recovered food. From the report, it was good to learn that governmental solutions to the problem were already underway. With the size of the bean pile in mind, however, it was clear to me that more efforts were necessary to solve the issue.

The unfortunate aspect was that these scalable government solutions deal with only one part of the problem, that of food *waste*, leaving the problem of food loss unaddressed by governments.

But with all our affluence, with all our smarts, the big question is:

Why?

CHAPTER 4

THE BIG FOOD WASTE QUESTIONS

———

Yes, why? When we can send people to the moon, build hand-held devices for wireless communication and driver-less cars, why can we not 'crack' the 'food waste nut'? Or, in the words of a Vox video, if "food waste is the world's dumbest problem," why can't we solve it?

In order to solve any problem, you have to understand the source. If you don't understand the source, you don't know where to begin to address it. So, what is the root cause or causes of the food waste problem in America? To get to this answer, my research led me to ask a number of other questions: questions of standards, predispositions, habits and more. I call these the BIG Food Waste Questions and they are as follows:

IS EXCESS OUR GUIDE?

Yes. One reason that America leads the food waste pack is that it has a culture of excess. When you look at America's waste as a whole, you will quickly see that food waste is just a piece of that pie. You also start to see a trend. "The United States leads the world in the production of waste, followed by other leading industrial nations. The U.S. manages to produce a quarter of the world's waste despite the fact that its population of 300 million is less than 5% of the world's population, according to 2005 estimates."[1]

WHAT IS 'UGLY'?

That's an ugly statistic, which brings me to the next question. What is 'imperfect' or, as we say more colloquially in the food world, 'ugly?' And who sets the standards?

As discussed at the outset, a lot of what gets wasted in the U.S. is a result of being considered 'imperfect' or 'ugly'. 'Ugly' produce includes our good friends, the dumped green beans. It also includes the two-legged carrot, a red pepper with a hunchback and a 'sun-tanned cauliflower.' Yes, in the world of cauliflowers, the snow-whiter the head, the better. And, unfortunately for the cauliflower, losing its 'whiteness' is pretty easy.

Cauliflowers grow above ground and, although they are shrouded in leaves when young, those leaves open as they mature, exposing them to the sun. And, if the exposure is too intense, they quickly become too 'tan'-looking and suffer the same fate as their irregular green cousin, the bean. In fact, after facing rejection at the produce section of our grocery stores, millions of sun-tanned cauliflower heads are now left to rot in fields in America each year. Their only crime: getting their tan on.

According to Jeshua King of Twin Springs Fruit Farm, which sells 'ugly' fruits and vegetables in addition to 'pretty' ones, there is great cost to farmers associated with food blemishes, which he affectionately called "blems." As a result, in order to reach fruit and vegetable perfection, most farmers that sell to grocery stores "spray every substance possible on their crop, be that fertilizer, fungicide, pesticide or other chemicals. They want to produce a perfect product and avoid blems at all costs. This is costly and environmentally damaging," he noted. King on the other hand is fortunate to sell all his produce directly to the consumer at farmer's markets. This enables his staff to educate the customers about the quality of ugly produce, allowing him to sell it rather than waste it.

So now that we know what ugly means, who is responsible for the waste resulting from discarding ugly produce? Who sets the beauty standards, so to speak? The grocery store or the consumer?

"As I first began to think about this issue," King said in an interview, "it seemed like a 'chicken and egg' dilemma. 95% of our customers still pick over every single apple and peach, looking for any little bruise, scarring or imperfection, which provides the reason not to purchase the food. Grocery stores cater to the wants of their customers in every which way. Hence the chicken and the egg."

But if you ask *me* who sets the standards, the answer is simple: We do. You and I, the consumers. The grocery stores and produce sellers are simply responding to *our* desires, to *our* beauty standards.

But that does not mean that grocery stores have no role to play in the food waste problem; they do, but it is a different one. The grocery business in the U.S. is a very refined and calculated model. It is geared towards trying to get the consumer to buy more than they can consume, which contributes to waste in and of itself. Try googling "grocery store psychology" and you'll see what I mean.

Grocery chains specifically design their stores to maximize sales. Everything from store layouts, to 'on sale' signs, to the music playing is carefully considered to make you buy more. Their marketing strategies encourage the exact opposite of what food-saving recommendations suggest, namely to buy only what you need. The stores encourage "impulse buys," by positioning products at the checkout counter or in bulk next to sales. As a result, consumers often purchase too much food and some of it spoils before they get around to eating it. In terms of layout, have you ever noticed how common staples, like milk, eggs and bread, are placed at the back of, or in the far corner of, the store? This way you will pass by every other department before you finally reach the staples, and along the way are teased to buy items you don't need and hadn't planned to buy.

Recently I noticed that the Whole Foods near my campus plays, wait for it... reggae music. I found this odd until I realized this was a well-researched decision regarding what music best matches the demographic served by this location. Whole Foods wants to lure young people in, put them in the best state of mind to buy and keep them there to listen to music they like so that they buy even more.

Here is a way to think about the food waste related to excess purchasing. In my mind, people treat food purchases like they do the prepaid time they buy on their monthly phone plans. They buy the maximum amount possible (hopefully for the minimum price) but don't make sure to maximize every last GB of data or every last minute of voice calls on their plan. They take a similar approach to food, forfeiting (or tossing) what is left over at the end of the month or week. The only difference is, wasting data or voice minutes does not cause the kinds of economic, social and environmental problems tossing out food does. And, to add insult to injury, we often toss things out that are perfectly edible.

WHAT'S IN A LABEL?

The issue of food labeling, another driver of food waste in the U.S. (and elsewhere for that matter) is also an interesting one. The main offenders are words such as 'sell by,' 'use by' or 'best by/before.' While intended to protect us in some way, these innocent words often result in avoidable waste. We treat the words as a fire alarm, a loud siren that causes us to dump everything whose time has come (or not) into the trash, no if's, and's or but's.

But, in reality, according to the website 'eatbydate.com,' "best by" dates are simply producer indications of the last date by which "a product's flavor and/or quality is at its best." It does not necessarily mean that the item is not fit for consumption either on or after that date. In fact, "most food is still edible after these printed expiration dates have passed." And, not only can food still be sold after the 'expiration date,' but food dates are not even required by law (except when it relates to baby formula).

All this to say that many perishable goods are perfectly edible past the labeled date. I know because I have eaten them. But, if you are not as daring as I am, some products approaching their "best by" date can be cooked for further preservation or frozen for later consumption. (I even froze cheddar cheese before a Christmas vacation once and melted it on chili when I returned.)

In an effort to reduce food waste, some groceries stores in Germany have made a business out of products that are nearing their best by dates. They have special sections and promotions (involving reduced pricing) and are finding willing customers. In the U.S., we are largely still too picky for this development.

WHY ARE WE SO PICKY?

This takes me to the next question. The way we ignore blemished food or dump products nearing their best by dates is an expression of how picky American society has become. If our iPhone has a scratch on it, we want a new one. If our sweater has a lose thread, we toss it out, and similarly, if our apple has a bruise on one side, we throw the whole fruit out. This doesn't speak for everyone, but still represents a staggering amount of people.

When my girlfriend was younger, her grandma scared her out of pickiness.

"The number of grains of rice you leave in the bowl represent the number of moles you'll grow," my girlfriend recalls her saying. As a young girl she was terrified of growing moles and thus terrified of squandering food that was perfectly good.

But through pickiness and quest for perfection, many American easily forget that advice. Somehow, we convince ourselves that the bruised apple doesn't taste as good as one without a blemish, or that green beans of a length less than three or more than five inches are inedible, or that sun-tanned cauliflowers are unsafe.

I now make an effort to live by the Taiwanese expression shared by my girlfriend's grandmother. It is not easy to do, especially when my girlfriend complains that the grapefruits I now buy from Hungry Harvest, an 'ugly food' delivery service, do not taste as good as the ones she buys at Whole Foods. While she may be right from time to time, I refuse to attribute this to where they came from or how they look, or to go back to my old habits of looking for the best-looking ones at a high-end grocer like Whole Foods Market. And as a result I still enjoy the grapefruit just as much.

DO WE JUST HAVE BAD HABITS?

That brings me to the topic of habits, which I will discuss more fully later. For consumers, one issue that drives food waste is that we are all creatures of habit. We do things we always did and eat things we always ate. Thinking along this line, I remembered the story of Norbert Wilson. As a student, he would buy jar after jar of pasta sauce. He would open one, then mindlessly another and another. He had every intention of using them up but "there's only so much spaghetti a person can eat." This meant "those jars occasionally ended up as half-eaten, fuzzy science experiments" lurking in the back of his refrigerator. Needless to say, he eventually tossed them out, another contribution to the food waste pile. Although a small example of food waste, this is one that stuck with him, making him question his lazy food habits, lazy habits we all have if we look a bit closer. Wilson is now a professor of food policy at the Friedman School of Nutrition Science and Policy.

IS CONVENIENCE CONVENIENT?

Our laziness also drives our fondness for convenience, which is another food waste problem. We look for things that are fast and easy, and when it comes to food, this also means prepared. In 2016, the food items posting the highest sales growth had one overarching theme in common: convenience (Nielsen). Below are the top three categories by sales growth:

- Refrigerated breakfast entrée (82.3% dollar sales growth)
- Frozen gravy and sauce (42.2%)
- Frozen meal starters (33.6%)

Convenience is growing in importance in many households. Just think of the growing assortment of prepared fresh food at your grocery store: perfect cubes of pre-sliced fruits, pre-minced/peeled garlic, packaged to perfection (Spoiler Alert: Watermelons and mangoes don't grow as rectangles. The scraps that are leftover to create these beautiful purchases often get tossed or composted if we are lucky.) Prepared foods are also the quickest foods to perish. In fact, veggie platters, pre-sliced food and other 'Prepared & Ready To Eat Meals' are "the most common food waste found in dumpsters." I learned this from William Reid, the world's most famous 'dumpster diver.' He should know, since he spent two years living off of nothing but food waste.

I recently called my local grocery store looking to see if they stocked a particular product. The computer answering service kindly offered to connect me with the top four most frequently requested departments. Catered and Prepared Foods were numbers 2 and 3, only after the pharmacy.

Back to Reid. He would have had it even easier in his dumpster diving days if he had met my cousin, Jerry. Convenience and fast food are near and dear to Jerry's heart; he is particularly fond of prepared meals: sandwiches, pasta dishes and soups to name a few. He has no time or interest in cooking. He just wants to pop things in his mouth or, at most, into the microwave. Like Norbert did as a student, he buys things he likes in bulk but, if he does not eat them in time, they end up in the trash. The fact that he follows 'best by' dates religiously just makes the food waste problem in his home even worse. Fortunately for Jerry, his family can afford and sustain his wasteful behavior, which brings me to the last question.

DOES MONEY BUY US WASTE?

Wealth or affluence is a contributor to food waste. Not surprisingly, developed countries (such Europe and the U.S.) thus waste significantly more at the consumer level than developing countries do. According to *Food Waste*, consumers in France, for example, waste 67% of the total 7.1 billion tons of the nation's food waste. And as seen by the facts cited earlier in this book, America, with its abundance of wealth, wastes more than its fair share of food as well.

In most developed countries, half of all food waste takes place in the home. People who live in poverty or in less developed societies simply can't afford to waste food. Their existence often depends on it. Food can play an important symbolic role as well. Just remember the proverb about what happens if you leave rice in your bowl.

CHAPTER 5

MY PROBLEM WITH FOOD WASTE

———

While I have never had to suffer due to a lack of rice in my bowl, my primary personal problem with food waste is societal. The negative environmental impacts also bother me and I dislike some of the factors I found while answering my BIG Food Waste Questions. The following assessments have been shaped by my experiences and observations I've made while living in several different countries and cultures.

SOCIETAL EFFECTS

The negative societal impact of food waste bothers me most. When I was living in Germany and attending elementary school, my favorite activity was going to McDonald's with my mom once a week after school. It was our secret (since my dad never would have approved) and that's what made it so special. I'd order fries, a box of chicken nuggets and apple juice and we'd take the same place on the red faux-leather benches by the window overlooking an old stone fountain. She'd tell me stories as I watched a little stone angel spit water out of his mouth into the pond below.

At the base of this pond, I always saw the same man, a homeless one with tattered clothes and an unkempt beard. His name was Gunther, I later found out. While I felt bad for him, I'd eat what I wanted from my meal and throw out what I didn't want when I was done. I was a kid and I just didn't associate my act with his condition. I just knew that I felt sorry for him.

Ever since then, however, the problem of homelessness has had a special place in my heart. And, as I grew older, I'd still throw out what I didn't want but whenever I passed Gunther or other beggars, I'd offer up whatever small amount of cash was in my wallet to help them out.

I continue to witness homelessness today as a student at Georgetown University, which is no surprise since D.C. has the fifth highest homeless population[1] and the third largest homelessness rate of any city in the United States, measured by the number of homeless people per 100,000 people[2]. The high cost of living in the nation's capital is to blame, according to *The New York Times*.

No longer a kid, and now aware of the link between food waste and hunger, it bothers me even more to see people in such a state. Students at Georgetown's dining hall leave plates half-full, while no more than a five-minute walk away a person experiencing homelessness is gong hungry. I cringe at the sight of the vast amounts of perfectly edible food that ends up in dumpsters as opposed to in the hands of those who could use it. The film *Just Eat It* really drove this message home for me. In the movie, its two producers Grant Baldwin and Jenny Rustemeyer showed how they could survive for six months mostly off of food found in a dumpster. They found tons of eggs and wrapped feta cheese that had been tossed well before the 'best before' dates. In the most shocking scene of the movie, the two producers found an entire dumpster six feet deep, full of sealed hummus tubs with three and a half weeks left prior to their 'best before' date.

I went dumpster diving myself once. Like Baldwin and Rustemeyer, I was not embarrassed. I didn't *need* to go on a scavenger hunt for food. It was part of my research. But it was sobering to think that there are many others out there that do need to dumpster dive for food *and* would not have to if we were not so wasteful, or at least did something better with our waste.

ENIVIRONMENTAL

The environmental impact of food waste, laid out in Chapter 1, also troubles me personally, particularly because we simply don't understand it. In other words, although more and more businesses and consumers say they are improving their environmental footprint, for example by using LED lighting, few are aware of the environmental damage they are causing with their food waste. For example, while we might turn off the tap while brushing our teeth, the damage caused by improperly discarding one pound of beef is the equivalent of taking a 370-minute shower!

Speaking of showers, if you are living on the east coast, access to fresh water is not a concern. The prospect is far bleaker in California, the fertile crescent of America. America relies on California to produce over a third of all its vegetables and two-thirds of the country's fruits and nuts[3]. Meanwhile, California recently went through one of its worst droughts in its recorded history, lasting from 2011 to 2017.[4] The biggest consumer of water in the U.S. is the agricultural industry, and if many of the fruits and vegetables it produces are also left to rot in fields, well that makes it a double whammy. According to one source, 25% of the nation's fresh water is wasted annually through America's food waste.[5]

This ignorance bothers me personally given my upbringing. My dad was always an adamant recycler and eco-conscious consumer. He's been buying organic food long before it became fashionable and was one of the first to join Princeton's Curbside Composting Pilot Program. (He's also been wearing one particular sweater for over 20 years and has been using the same leather work bag for the last 35.) I credit him for my values of sustainability and I try to live by them as much as possible. Whether it's riding my bike everywhere, using a refillable water bottle or recycling religiously, it is my dad I am trying to emulate. Even my vegetarian diet (like his) is eco-friendly. Just in case you did not know, animal products require a lot more resources to produce than plants: one serving of grass-fed beef produces 330 grams of carbon dioxide, while one serving of lentils produces only 2 grams!

OTHER FACTORS (FROM THE BIG FOOD WASTE QUESTIONS)

The problem of excess is something I definitely encountered when I moved from Germany to America. The obsession with XXL in everything from cars to soft drinks, was a cultural shock that I never quite came to terms with. Even the refrigerators in America are much bigger than those in Europe. To add insult to injury, a lot of the Americans I met even have a second large refrigerator or a huge freezer in the garage as well! Given this obsession with excess, it is no wonder that the food waste problem in America is also XXL.

As for the concept of 'ugly' fruits and vegetables and the desire to seek out the nicer-looking ones, well that spans both continents I've lived in. That said, I always found myself picking out the lopsided apples or deformed squash. Maybe I just like weird things or maybe I really did learn from the stories my mother told me at McDonald's: "You should not judge a book by its cover." Later in life, I learned a lesson or two about judging bruises (or at least bruised peaches). For more on this story, read on.

PART 2

MY FOOD
WASTE
JOURNEY

CHAPTER 6

A FOOD WASTE
SELF-ASSESSMENT

———

MY ONION-INSPIRED EPIPHANY

Princeton is one of the most beautiful places to experience fall. I know, because I spent most of my childhood growing up there. Looking down upon this central part of New Jersey from the sky, it looks like a forest, not a town. An occasional line cuts through the trees, a road connecting the homes, which themselves are shrouded by green foliage. In autumn, however, the area around my house looks less like a forest and more like a painter's palette; a wild mix of maroon, yellow, orange and green paint the canvas I call home. My favorite way to enjoy this scenery is by riding my bike, getting lost in the unpredictable blend of colors, while remembering to look down every once in a while to avoid fallen branches and, of course, the potholes.

Two years ago, a few days before Thanksgiving, I decided to prepare lunch before heading out for a ride. I wanted to make my favorite dish: *Pasta al pomodoro*, pasta cooked to al dente perfection and coated lightly in a silky, naturally sweet *Sugo di Pomodoro*. In layman's terms, noodles with tomato sauce! It's such a simple dish but, when it comes together just right, it's hard to beat. My favorite sauce comes from the recipe of Marcella Hazan. Her particular recipe owes its famous flavor to its "low and slow" simmer preparation and its three simple ingredients: butter, onion, and *D.O.P. San-Marzano* tomatoes, a protected variety grown only in the fertile, volcanic-ash soil at the foothills of Mount Vesuvius, an active volcano in Italy.

The preparation took no time at all. The hour-long wait for the sauce to develop its flavor provided an added benefit: it gave me just enough time to get some fresh air and exercise on my two wheels. After having simmered for over an hour, by the time I returned, I saw the trusted sign that the sauce was done: the butter fat had completely emulsified and the sauce had developed a deep red hue, indicating it had reduced to the right consistency. Having made this recipe countless times, my hands now moved unconsciously, boiling the water, and cooking the noodles in preparation for a glorious matrimony between pasta and sauce.

As I walked toward the compost bin, saucepot in hand, I repeated the last step of the recipe in my head: *Discard the onion before tossing the sauce with pasta.* Almost robotically, I spooned out the onion halves and lifted the lid of the compost bin and then...

I hesitated.

I hesitated at a step of my routine that I had executed so many times in the past that it had become a habit. This time, when I paused briefly to look at what I was about to throw away, my inner voice spoke, cried almost.

"Why don't you eat these? They look good!"

Truth be told, I had considered eating the onion halves several times in the past but always assumed they would be tasteless and mushy, much like tea leaves after steeping in hot water. After all, they had already imparted all their flavor to the medium they had cooked in.... Or hadn't they?

Only one way to find out, I thought as I redirected the spoon to my mouth, squinting my eyes in anticipation of a fibrous, bland ghost of what the vegetable had once been.

I chewed and paused to fully absorb the sensations I experienced:

Soft...

Silky!

Sweet!!

To my pleasant surprise, the onion was as delicious as the sauce itself! I was amazed by my discovery and rushed back to my computer to share it with the rest of the food world! *Slow your roll there, Adrian*, I said to myself. *You may be not be the first to make this discovery.* And, surely enough, by scrolling through the comments of The New York Times Cooking website, where I had first found the recipe, I quickly discovered that I was not the "Onion Pioneer."

"That's the best part. I'll eat that all by itself if I have to, or puree it into its own sauce with a little roasted garlic to spread on some good bread."

(By the way, I followed this creative suggestion some weeks later. Delicious!)

"Eating it is one of the highlights of this dish!"

(I would recreate the same experience a few months later when I prepared handmade ricotta gnocchi and this sauce for my girlfriend's family in Taiwan. They loved the gnocchi, and the sauce, but most of all, appreciated the onions, helping themselves to seconds and thirds. Several times that night my girlfriend's Po-po (grandmother) nudged her and said "可以把洋蔥遞給我嗎?" meaning, "Can you pass me more onion, please?" in Mandarin.

As someone who loves cooking, but still has a lot to learn, I attribute my moderate culinary talent to my extensive Internet research and my careful selection of recipes, which I follow religiously. I attribute my first personal lesson in food waste prevention, on the other hand, to altering a recipe: not following it religiously and actually thinking about what I put into a dish and what I (unconsciously) throw out. This onion-inspired experience triggered a food waste epiphany and marked the start of my drive to reduce food waste!

ME BEFORE ME—A FOOD WASTE SELF-ASSESSMENT

I'm starting with the man in the mirror. I'm asking him to change his ways.

—MICHAEL JACKSON

Having researched the problem of food waste—facts, figures, issues, terminology and reasons—and having had my onion epiphany, I thought it might make sense to take a closer look at my personal contribution to the problem before making further changes and starting to proselytize to friends and family. I decided to approach the issue *à la* Michael Jackson.

Unfortunately, the speckled mirror in my college dorm room provided little enlightenment. And so, I turned instead to the key to all wisdom: the Internet. That's where I found (and took) a number of online food waste quizzes to see if they could give me some further insight into my habits.

One test result indicated I was *"moderately mindful."*

Hmm. Not bad! I thought, feeling a sense of satisfaction, until I realized I was some way from the top category of *"Food Rescue Rockstar."*

Nevertheless, I found the quizzes useful; they made me aware of some general good food habits. Unfortunately, however, they didn't provide me with a concrete understanding of *what* I wasted and *why* I did so. From my research into habits and changing them (read on for more), I knew I had to have a better awareness and understanding of myself before I went any further.

That is when I decided to perform a real food-waste assessment, an analysis that would also establish a baseline from which I could set goals and track my progress. Fortunately for me, the US Environmental Protection Agency (EPA) had just the thing: *"A Guide to Conducting and Analyzing a Food Waste Assessment."* (For more information on what governmental organizations and agencies are doing to help fight food waste, see Part III).

Although the EPA Guide is tailored to organizations and businesses, I used it as a model to develop my own assessment tool, a four-step guide, which works as follows:

1. Historical Analysis: a.k.a picking through my trash;
2. Logging: recording the food waste I produced during a weeklong period;
3. Analysis: analyzing amounts and reasons given for the waste and whether they are valid;
4. Record Benefits: of wasting less.

Before starting the assessment, I also purchased (or secured) the following, which I thought I would be essential:

- Compost bucket and bags
- Gloves with forearm sleeves for picking through the trash. (Mine are pink!)
- A strong stomach and nose—old food scraps can become both unsightly and smelly!
- Big dose of dedication. This was going to be a lot of work, particularly for a busy college student juggling classes, job applications, and writing a book (the one you're holding).

And voila, my personal results:

1. HISTORICAL ANALYSIS

In order to have a large enough "sample" for the historical analysis, I needed to wait until the trash was full. (I also needed to wait for some alone-time, as the sight of me rummaging through our trash might have shocked my roommates, particularly those who may not have #3 on my supply list.)

As soon as the coast was clear, I slipped on my pink rubber gloves, and sorted through the trash, one item at a time, looking for my personal contributions. The odor was bearable at first, but when I reached my roommate's half-eaten chicken wings, the smell was so overwhelming I almost added a clothespin to my list.

Back to my food waste: it consisted of unopened expired yogurt cups, leftover slices of pizza, an overripe avocado, a piece of stale baguette, and a mountain of wilted, pre-washed salad leaves. At the time, it was too late to rescue any of it but looking back upon this later, I realized I could have prevented every single one of these items from landfill destiny.

Taking both my and my roommate's food into account, I quickly determined that 50% of the bag was food, an amount that is worse than the already shocking national level of 21%.

Thankfully, I contributed the least to this amount but the analysis allowed me to confirm my suspicion that one particular roommate—the former owner of the chicken wings—belongs in criminal food waste court!

With a newfound appreciation for those working with waste, I was ready to move on to phase 2, logging.

2. LOGGING

If you've ever tried logging your every meal while dieting, you know what a pain it can be. You either forget (or want to), or do it all after the fact and in a rush. Logging every single food item you throw out is not any more exciting.

My assessment week nevertheless started off strong. On Monday, I threw any food I didn't want into a separate compostable bin and recorded the amount. I home-cooked many of my meals that week, which explains the large quantities of items tossed each day. These were a few of them:

- 1/3 of a can of coconut milk. Reason: Gross! Rancid.
- A piece of cucumber. Reason: Gross! Mushy and slimy.
- Three zucchini tops. Reason: Inedible. Too hard to eat.
- Banana peels. Reason: Inedible.
- Etc.

Tuesday's logging ran smoothly as well and my list included:

- One parmesan rind. Reason: Inedible.
- Couple of handfuls of wilted, mushy pre-washed salad leaves: Reason: Gross! Slimy.
- Slice of Paleo banana bread (gift from friend): Reason: Gross! Tasteless.
- Citrus peels. Reason: Inedible.
- Wrinkled, soft grapes. Reason: Unappealing!
- Etc.

The rest of the week continued similarly—sometimes with my having to fish out the food from the normal trash and place it into my compost bin—but on Saturday something changed. I was preparing to toss and record another item—kale stems. Reason: Inedible. Fibrous—I thought about my onion epiphany. Maybe cooking would soften them up?

"Hmmm. I wonder if they can be eaten after all," I thought.

And Google's clear answer: Yes! A Bon-Àppetit article offered a plethora of creative ways to prepare this secret ingredient, but I opted for the easiest one—*Sauté*—and the result was delicious.

Sunday marked the day with my highest amount of waste, but that was because I felt inspired to do a fridge cleanup. I found many items, which I had to toss, or so I thought at the time, and others that I could save and, with a bit of research, enjoy.

3. ANALYZE RESULTS

During phase three, I reflected on the process and analyzed the results. The assessment, though burdensome, was very successful. Additionally, one factor played a particularly important role for me personally. During a corporate EPA assessment, the people producing the food waste are not the same as those doing the sorting, logging or analysis. I, however, was wearing all hats, so the resulting awareness was more tangible.

An analysis of my logs revealed the causes of my waste and which ones were most significant. The #1 reason I threw out food was because I determined it was "inedible". As I learned on the Saturday of phase two, however, something "inedible" could be made edible with the right technique and a bit of effort. (This continued to be a theme throughout my journey as I learned to cook with broccoli stems, carrot tops, citrus peels and more.)

The #2 reason I tossed food was that it was "gross!" Except for the banana bread which was really bad (trust me), all of the food I found too "gross" or unappealing to eat, was at one point perfectly good. I just did not prioritize eating it in time or had too much food in the fridge at once to recognize what needed to be eaten first and what could wait. Constantly maintaining an abundant variety in my fridge was causing me to waste food.

Suffice it to say that this exercise allowed me to see what, when and why I was producing food waste, which allowed me to be more conscious of my actions. And, given that awareness was the goal of this exercise, I would say: Mission accomplished!

4. BENEFITS

My assessment not only provided awareness, but also some immediate benefits such as fewer trips to the store, less trash to carry out (especially when I started salvaging my room-mates' food or telling them what to eat next), not to mention less stress on my wallet. I learned more about what could be composted, and how and where (more on this in Part III).

That said, the awareness was the most fundamental bene-fit. It not only provided the basis I needed for change going forward, but it also piqued my curiosity to understand more, particularly as this awareness related to the heritage of food waste prevention that my mother so often referred to. For this, I went back to old stories and old experiences, and the addi-tional knowledge I gained helped propel me forward.

CHAPTER 7

A FAMILY OF FOOD WASTE WARRIORS

———

IT'S IN THE GENES

By the next Thanksgiving, after a year of trying to change my behavior, I was making progress and my genetic predisposition to reduce food waste was beginning to emerge. This fact came to light very publicly after dinner at one of my family's favorite restaurants, the Dosa Grill. Getting to the restaurant involves an hour round-trip ride to and from our house. On a weeknight, that sort of commute is enough to convince most families to eat at home, dine somewhere else, or just order in, but Dosa Grill has a special place in each of our Indian-food-loving hearts. And so, whenever we are all together, we'll pile into the car and make the long trek there at least once.

Arriving in the dark of night, as we usually do, it's very easy to miss this small hole in the wall, located in a nondescript mini-mall along a highway in central New Jersey. The crowd at the door is, however, a reliable signpost: day or night, the entrance is always packed in the best sort of way. The patrons are 95% of Indian descent, always a good indicator of quality ethnic cuisine in my book.

While we've been there many times, we are still exploring the extensive menu so we often order after being inspired by (and asking) what people are eating at the neighboring tables. That is how we were introduced to Dahi Vada—soft lentil dough-nuts soaked in a deliciously mild yogurt sauce.

The Dahi Vada, which are now my father's favorite thing on the menu, and the other dishes we had were delicious and plentiful. So much so, that at the end of the meal, there was a lot of food left over—another opportunity to reduce food waste in my eyes! Since my onion experience the year before, I had not only made a conscious effort to reduce food waste in the process of cooking, but also adopted new anti-food-waste habits such as salvaging leftovers for later enjoyment.

And so, at the end of our meal, I asked the waiter if we could take all the leftovers to go. While this is as common a request in this local restaurant as it is in any other, on this occasion, the waiter quickly learned that my definition of *all* was not so common.

He started by bringing out three small styrofoam containers for our remains and I began to salvage. I strategically filled each one, first laying down a base of white rice, onto which I stacked folded Dosas and Uthappams. But there was more food I could not leave behind. I needed bowls for the leftover Sambar and Rasam, which he graciously gave me. But when I asked for containers for the mango lassi, a yogurt drink, and the many delicious, half-full chutneys, it was clear he had met his "doggie bag" match.

In fact, he looked at me, amused by my unusual request, raised his eyebrows and said to my parents, "He's really hardcore, eh?"

"I know!" My mom replied, shaking her head, partly amused and partly embarrassed. By that point in my food-packing-extravaganza, we had gathered an audience. And, as Mom saw me scraping the plates and bowls, in an effort to save every last grain of biriyani rice and every last drop of coconut chutney, she had another family flashback.

"Oh Adrian... You really are just like my *Nonno!*"

My desire and diligence to save all this food reminded my mother of her maternal grandfather again.

"How?" I asked, anxious for another good story.

"Well suffice it to say that the only difference is that, instead of asking for containers, he would have eaten the rest, whether hungry or not. He didn't like to waste a single crumb, not even the soggy ones."

This was another indication that my passion to reduce food waste was in the genes. But I would have to dig deeper to understand the depth of these roots.

CHAPTER 8

FOOD AND WAR: A HISTORY LESSON

———

THE LINK BETWEEN WAR AND FOOD

Not surprisingly, digging deeper into my family's past and my Italo-German heritage led me to the topic of war—a common thread on both sides of the family tree. And war led me back to food, specifically how it was valued during wartime and consequently how it was treated. (Remember the experiences of my German grandfather?)

America also has a history of war, including the two world wars. As a result, in the course of my research, it was not surprising that I found a link between food and war closer to home as well. What was surprising, however, at least to me, were some of the facts I discovered along the way.

One interesting finding was the association between the U.S. Food and Drug Administration (USFDA) and war. Like my grandfather, the FDA also developed some great and time-less food waste reduction tips, only they disseminated theirs publicly and intentionally.

During World War I, the agency was responsible for the administration of food reserves to the U.S. army overseas as well as the Allies.

One particular poster it developed in this era struck a nerve with me. It was simply entitled "food":

The last two points in particular brought a pleasant reminder of my grandparents, the ones who cooked sparingly and ate everything, and often out of the same pot. ;-)

Another thing I learned lessened the smile on my face, and that was that these simple words of wisdom have largely been forgotten. Affluence and increased standards of living have caused us to celebrate abundance, variety and choice, and consequently to be more wasteful in the process. As I read and re-read these six simple rules for behavior, I realized just how much I valued their brevity and clarity. And while they are 'old' words, I could not help but think how topical and relevant they still are. In fact, they are so concise, they would even be short enough to tweet!

And that made me think: if these six points played a role in helping the U.S. win WWI, then we could and *should* 'enlist' them again to win the war against food waste.

This was a powerful and surprising discovery. At a time in our nation's history when 70.7% of the American population is classified as overweight or obese, it's hard to imagine a nationwide effort where the majority of Americans voluntarily restrict their diets to free up food to send overseas [Centers for Disease Control, 2014]. But millions of Americans did just that during WWI. Below are some of the posters circulated by the United States government in that era.

don't waste food
while others starve!

UNITED STATES FOOD ADMINISTRATION

Food *is*
Ammunition-
Don't waste it.

don't
let
up

Keep On
Saving Food

"We are saving you
YOU save FOOD"

Well fed Soldiers
WILL WIN the WAR

Other posters, not featured here, further encouraged citizens to save food with dramatic words: "Food will win the war" and "Every spoonful—and every sip—means less for a fighter." They all very clearly reflect the dark and serious nature of that period in world history and the implications it had for our relationship with food.

Between now and then, or put another way, somewhere along the way between my grandparents and me, the precious value of food diminished. As the generations distanced themselves from war, from scarcity and from poverty, food waste started to creep in. I was determined to go back to these times, not to war, but to a time when food was valued. And so I decided to go back to my roots, not only figuratively, but also geographically.

CHAPTER 9

SMALL STEPS AND BIG ONES TOO

MY PERSONAL FOOD WASTE ODYSSEY

It was the summer after my sophomore year of high school. My family had moved back to Europe for a short time and I decided to visit them and spend time in Europe in the process. The first destination on my list was Naples, the birthplace of my grandmother and my maternal grandparents.

With both a passion for food and the gene for preventing food waste already in my blood, my travels across the globe turned out to be my very own unexpected food waste odyssey. Two particular experiences, which could not have been a starker contrast, shaped me and allowed me to take several steps forward in my food waste journey.

It all started when I decided to become a *Pizzaiolo*, Italian for 'Official Neapolitan Pizza Maker"—yes that designation actually exists. (That said, I quickly learned that *Pizzaiolo* is a title you earn long after passing the course, so while on Italian soil, I called myself a *Pizzaiolo* 'novice' so as not to offend the real ones.)

I signed up for the course after hearing my Aunt Ida's rave review of the one she'd taken the year before. She tickled my curiosity with funny pictures of her time there: one of her dressed in the traditional, all white, *Pizzaiolo* uniform, one with steamy Pizza Pie in hand and one complete with sweaty handkerchief. (I would soon learn just how important that seemingly useless cloth was. Suffice it to say that, in the peak of the southern Italian summer, the small classroom filled with 15 people and two 1,000°F ovens gets hot, hot, hot.)

The course was offered by the "Associazione Verace Pizza Napoletana," the True Neapolitan Pizza Association, and I spent three weeks in Naples, perfecting the art of pizza-making. It was a phenomenal, not to mention delicious, experience that ended up also really opening my eyes to the issue of food waste.

Our cohort that summer was all male, but we were still an extremely diverse bunch. We hailed from all over the globe: Japan, Australia, Portugal. Even Norway and Germany—the lands of my ancestors—were represented. Despite five different languages being spoken at all times, we somehow managed to understand each other.

The class ended up being as much about pizza-making as it was about understanding the ingredients and the equipment itself. We went on many field trips, for example to visit a commercial flour mill on the outskirts of Naples, or to an artisan oven factory in the heart of the city in an old, gutted police station. In class, we learned everything from flour properties to how to properly knead and shape dough to how to choose the right toppings. We even had the opportunity to spend a week and a half outside of class working in a certified Italian Pizzeria. As luck would have it, I got placed at the *Antica Pizzeria Port'Alba*. Located on an cobbled path branching off from the Piazza Bellini, it sits nestled into the bottom floor of an old stone building. Shrouded by the shade of the arch above, its appearance is unassuming, so I didn't think much of it. It wasn't until I told my classmates and saw their slightly jealous reaction that I found out I was 'interning' at what is widely believed to be the world's oldest pizzeria.

After a crash course in Italian, I got right to work in the school kitchen and soon enough I was making pizza after pizza, honing my skills more and more each day. By the end of the three-week course, I had made so many delicious pies, I could not believe my own eyes. The other thing my eyes could not believe, though, was just how many of them, including mine, we were throwing out in the process. As the weeks progressed, what I learned most of all was how much I hated seeing the waste. We cranked out pie after pie, stacking them up on the table in the center of the class for our teachers to quickly scrutinize, looking for a round shape, a puffy crust, and little flour on the bottom—and then toss. At the end of each day, we produced a large garbage pail full of our misshapen, imperfect but otherwise perfectly delicious pizzas. The garbage was so full, you could see crusts hanging out of the edge! In a sea of memories about Naples, memories of old cobblestone streets and delicious food, this dark scene was by far the most memorable and for all the wrong reasons. (This was particularly the case because, before arriving in Europe for this course, I had spent three weeks in Ghana teaching entrepreneurship to young Ghanaian students and all I could think was what many there would have given to eat our leftovers…)

And so, while I got my official designation and learned Italian in the process, I left Naples a bit disillusioned about the food business. While learning to make pizza and working in a food kitchen, I saw firsthand just how much good food goes to waste. It was a travesty.

The next and most decisive step in my food waste journey was a big one. From Naples, I went work as a WWOOFer on a small organic farm on the outskirts of Toulouse. WWOOF is a worldwide movement linking volunteers, like me, with organic farmers and is aimed at building a sustainable, global community. (See http://www.wwoof.net for more information.)

It was there that I had the ultimate food waste experience. I lived in simple quarters with seven other WWOOFers from all over the world. Each morning we'd have to be up and standing outside the barn at 6 am. (Not a great time for a night owl like me.) From there Mr. Potier, the farm owner, delegated us to work in the various fields where we performed duties such as watering, pruning and harvesting until early afternoon, breaking only for water or trips to the market to sell our goods.

One day, after a long session in the sun harvesting peaches, I was surprised to find I had more energy left in me. As the others returned to their beds for an afternoon *siesta,* I decided to do Mr. Potier a favor by sorting through the day's harvest. Hunched over a few stacks of crates, filled with freshly picked peaches, I merrily sorted through them, robotically separating the bad ones from the good. By the time I was done, the sound of the farm dog barking alerted me to the fact that Mr. Potier was returning from the fields. I became very excited to show him what I had done for him. As the low rumble of the old tractor engine came to a halt, I suddenly heard Mr. Potier shout, in French:

"What the hell do you think you're doing!" He dismounted and marched over to the pile of fruit on the floor. "Why are those peaches on the floor? Arrete!" he said, stopping me from discarding the next one.

"But I am separating the good ones from the bad ones," I explained, innocently.

"*Mais, Non!*" he protested. "These are all perfectly good peaches! Even this one," he said, picking up one with a big, wet, almost moldy bruise that I'd placed in the reject pile. "All you have to do is this."

He whipped out his pocket-knife and carved out the brown spot, revealing the beautiful orange flesh beneath. Then he said, "Voila! Even this part has use." He pointed to the spotty bit he'd just cut out before placing it in the compost bin.

I was completely taken aback by the experience. It was not until later that night, lying in bed, that I realized that despite saving boiled onions, despite being educated by green beans, despite salvaging leftovers like a madman and despite having just been appalled by trashcan after trashcan of perfectly edible pizzas, my approach to food had just been fundamentally challenged, proving to me that I still had a long way to go.

I felt so guilty about having upset my generous host by almost wasting the literal 'fruits of his labor' that I couldn't fall asleep. After tossing and turning in self-reflection, I felt the best way to redeem myself was by offering a sincere apology but, more importantly, by changing my behavior. Yes, by changing certain unconscious, deeply ingrained food habits I still had. What I didn't know at the time, however, was that this determination would eventually lead to a profound change to how I lived. Not only that, it would lead to a newfound appreciation, respect in fact, for food.

The Food Waste Warrior seed, already in my genes, had been generously watered by this experience.

The next day when we returned to the orchard to harvest more peaches, I spent it on all fours, picking up every fallen, bruised one, laying them gently in the crates and appreciating their value. I even saw the beauty in the ugly ones.

The next few weeks on the farm were all about making the most of what the land gave to us, and living off the proceeds of selling the bounty. And so, when we ate potatoes, we fried the skins for snacks. When we had apple scraps, we made apple butter to sell at the weekly market. In other words, when life gave us lemons, we literally made lemonade! By the end of the third week, I was committed in every sense of the word. I saw the power of food, the value it could bring and how little really had to go to waste. And speaking of waste, believe it or not, during the entirety of the three-week stay, the seven farm volunteers produced a grand total of one half of a bag of real garbage. *ONE HALF* in case you missed that! Compare this to your weekly household garbage production and you will realize just how impressive this accomplishment is.

These experiences, my personal experiences, set me off on my very own FWW path. It is a path I have embraced and will continue to travel, not only because I see the commercial value in it, but also because I see the good in it. These steps I took, big and small, led me not only to realizations and commitments but also unknowingly to writing this book. For the book, however, two more things were necessary: additional research into my past and developing a process to move forward.

CHAPTER 10

BACK TO THE ROOTS AGAIN

———

FAMILY OF FOOD WASTE WARRIORS

A few weeks later, I was back on the Hilltop for my junior year. Classes had started and I was back to the grind, which found me studying at Georgetown University's Law Center Library, a 30-minute bike ride from campus.

Walking into the picturesque reading room always feels like I've stepped into a scene from Harry Potter: the quintessential high ceiling, the tall glass windows and the dark wood tables lined with incandescent lamps and heavy chairs always remind me of the dining room of Hogwarts, minus flying brooms and talking hats. In the Georgetown Law Library, those are replaced by the white noise of fingers clacking on keyboards, pencils scribbling, and pages turning; a productive hum that makes me feel smarter just listening to it!

As beautiful as the Georgetown campus is, I'd often drag myself off of it in an effort to escape "The Georgetown Bubble." And, I was not the only one to do so. The practice of "Breaking The Bubble" has quite a large following, namely in the form of a club by the same name, a club that recognizes the importance of leaving the microcosm of the main campus in order to feel reconnected to the outside world.

The Law Center Library was always one of my favorite destinations to escape to and open my mind. In addition to this, I always hoped that the work ethic and knowledge of the diligent law students would somehow rub off on me. Often it does, but, on this particular day, the magic wasn't working. A spell of distraction had been cast on me and my mind kept drifting away from multiple linear regression and back to Dosa Grill, the warm pot of Pasta al Pomodoro, pizza-making and farm life. I kept thinking about the commitment I'd made and how I was going to keep it.

Looking up at the old books and records in the library somehow reminded me of my family history and I was overwhelmed by the desire to learn more about it, particularly as it related to food waste.

And although libraries are normally fantastic places to do research, there would be no mention of my German-Italian ancestors and their relation to food waste in the bound volumes that surrounded me. No book or skilled librarian would be able to help me with these questions either. Instead I had to turn to one of the best recorders of my family history: my Aunt, Ida Albo.

I was so anxious for answers, that I decided to contact her then and there.

"Hi Ida," I texted. "I'm writing a book on food waste and want to learn more about our family's experience with this subject. Can I call you sometime to ask you some questions?" *Send.*

My aunt is a kind soul and had helped me often in the past, so I felt confident she would not only respond positively and quickly, but would also be a great help. (The fact that she was a successful owner of several restaurants, and an authority on food, was a bonus.)

And sure enough, a few minutes later my phone buzzed. "Sure! How about now?"

As mentioned, I was in a library, a place where silence was the rule but I found myself exclaiming "Yes!" out loud, before I could stop it. Slightly embarrassed, I moved to a secluded place and called.

After exchanging pleasantries, she asked, "So how can I help? What do you want to know?"

I briefly explained the issue of food waste, the comparison my mom had drawn between her grandfather and me, and the questions these topics raised about our family history. She laughed at my mom's comments and provided some insight of her own.

"Your mom's right! Your great-grandpa notoriously hated wasting anything." She paused briefly to recollect, then continued. "I remember him reaching into the fridge once and drinking milk that'd gone sour, straight out of the carton. In fact, I even remember him pouring me a glass but I passed after I smelled it. Ew did it smell sour!" My mind flashed back to the farm and the bruised peaches. Eating them, bruise and all, paled in comparison to this. Ida tore me from my thoughts. "He reassured me the milk was fine. I definitely didn't want to try it but he could not bring himself to pour it down the drain."

I laughed hesitantly at the story.

"Your mom wasn't as lucky though!"

"Huh? What do you mean?"

"It was a very hot summer so we had gone to our grandparents' house to cool off inside. We were really hungry too, having played outside all day, so we went in to have a snack. Our *Nonna*, our mother's mother, made us tuna sandwiches and poured us all some milk—the fresh kind! Your mom, as usual, got carried away with talking and all of a sudden dropped part of her sandwich into the glass of milk!"

"…aaand?" I asked.

"What do you mean 'aaand?' Our grandpa made her eat the sandwich *and* drink the milk of course! After her sandwich fell in, it became *hers* and she was responsible for its consumption."

"Oh God!" I said, contorting my face at the thought of that soggy sandwich.

"Yeah. As you can imagine, your other aunt, Belinda, and I held onto our slices very tightly after that." She started laughing and so did I.

"Another time, I think it was the following summer—I can't exactly remember—we were at our grandparents' house for lunch. Once again, we had been playing outside for hours and had developed quite an appetite, right in time to be called inside to eat. My grandparents always had large bottles of 7-Up in the fridge and poured us each a glass: a real treat in those days. And can you guess who spilled her soda?"

"My mom?" I responded with amusement, the way every child feels when they learn about an embarassing story in their parent's past.

"Yep! Our *Nonno* got up, walked to the drawer and grabbed a clean towel. He wiped all the soda off of the table, carried the dripping towel back to the sink, set down a glass, and wrung out the towel right into the glass. This time he drank it, even though it was your mother's '*responsibility.*'"

"Wow…" My voice trailed off. By this point in the conversation, I was starting to find my great-grandfather's actions off-putting, as you, readers, also might.

"Ida, you talk about the things he did so 'matter-of-factly,' almost as if wringing out a dish cloth and drinking the drippings is a normal thing to do."

"Well Adrian," she said, taking on a more serious tone than before, "your great-grandfather grew up in a very different time and place. Growing up in extreme poverty in southern

Italy is very different than it is for you growing up in the US today. To him, those were just ways he learned to survive."

"I guess you're right." I paused briefly to reflect. "But, by those measures you must think that my generation is more wasteful than previous ones?"

"Of course!" she insisted. "*HE* went without. *YOU* don't go without anything." Although the words were clear, I was curious to hear more.

"Could you elaborate?" I nudged.

"Nowadays, when your generation wants something they can get it at a push of a button. There's too much choice and convenience for you to want to eat leftovers, let alone sour milk. You open the fridge and say 'What do I want to eat?' You see the pizza from last night and think 'Oh but I ate that yesterday' and so you get a kebab delivered for five bucks on Uber Eats and, even then, you only eat half. You have so much variety and accessibility. You did not grow up needy so you don't think the same way our grandfather did."

"That's true," I agreed. "But what about your generation then? You didn't grow up with Uber Eats. Does it waste as much as mine does?"

"No it doesn't. But I'm not perfect either, because I grew up with more than my parents and their parents did. I also sometimes don't feel like eating my leftovers or cooking with what I have, so I just go to a restaurant. It's a defining characteristic of my more affluent generation. My grandpa's generation—mired by war, poverty and scarcity—developed a way of life and habits that wasted virtually nothing. Your grandpa, my father, lived a better life so his routines wasted a little more, but certainly less than me. I have prospered even more, also because of my parents, so I waste more than they did. Thanks to today's rapidly developing economy and better quality of life, your generation has developed habits that are more wasteful than mine. The question is, will the next generation after you waste even more, or will they reverse the cycle?"

FAMILY OF FOOD WASTE WARRIORS— THE NEXT GENERATION

My aunt left me with that question ringing in my ears. Were things just going to get worse? Or could my generation, could I, put a stop to this? I had no clue. The only thing I did know was that I wanted to learn more. I needed more context, so I called my mother.

I kicked off the conversation by telling her that I had just heard the story about her unfortunate encounter with a milk-soaked tuna sandwich that she was forced to eat. While this was not a pleasant memory, the story fortunately brought back other, better food waste related memories, this time involving her parents, *my Nonno* and *Nonna*.

My grandparents moved to Canada in the 1950's and, like many immigrants of their day, eventually started a business. In their case it was a grocery store, which bore their name: Albo Meats and Groceries. My mother grew up in her parents' store—well more precisely in the apartment on top of the store. Their whole life revolved around food and the Italian community the grocery store largely served.*

Whenever my sisters and I complained about having to empty the dishwasher or put our clothes in the laundry bin (instead of leaving them all over the floor where *we* thought they belonged), my mom would remind us that she'd had to work at the store from the time she had hand-eye coordination. We'd start rolling our eyes every time she mentioned those words. She would nevertheless go on to tell us how she had begun by stocking shelves, then moved up to bagging groceries and eventually made her way working behind the till (to cash people out) and then behind the wheel (to deliver groceries). Given all the time she spent at the store, she definitely had relevant stories to tell.

---

* The fact that Italians were their target clientele was less a strategic decision than one made out of necessity: my grandparents spoke very little English when they started out and my nonno still speaks with a very thick Italian accent when he speaks English. Sometimes when talking to him, I don't know if he is speaking Italian or English.)

"So, mom, growing up in the grocery store, you have got to have some food waste stories of your own, right? "

"I do! I just don't know where to start." She paused briefly. "Oh, yes, I've got one—the Tomato Lady!"

"The Tomato Lady?" I repeated.

"Yes, my parents had a hard time remembering everyone's name, so they would call them by what they did instead of what their parents named them. The Player's Tobacco* guy was also a regular customer for example."

I chuckled.

"Well anyway, I remember the Tomato Lady vividly because it was the first time I saw my dad get angry with a customer. She would come in every week to buy tomatoes to make her tomato sauce, but this weekly exercise became less a grocery shopping excursion than a lab examination."

"Hmmm? I'm lost Mom."

"Well Tomato Lady's tomatoes had to be 'juuust right,' just like Goldilock's bed in the story with the three bears. At first,

---

* Player's Tobacco is an old Tobacco brand.

she just picked them up, held them close to her nose and inhaled but, with time, she got stranger and stranger. She'd start squeezing them and prodding them with her thumb, often breaking the skins and then leaving them on the pile as if they were 'unworthy' of her sauce. Needless to say, this left a lot of unsalable tomatoes for my parents. No one wants to buy a tomato with a hole in it."

I could hear my mom move her arms as she imitated the lady and I laughed out loud.

"One day, my dad caught her, 'red-handed' so to speak. It started out friendly enough but descended rapidly, very quickly. 'Listen, lady,' he said, 'if you come to my store you do me a favor, but, if you don't come, you do me two! Your business costs me more than it is worth!' We did not see much of her after that visit."

I laughed again, but then I caught myself. The tomato-lady's quest for the 'perfect tomato' may seem a little ridiculous, but it's actually not that far from America's current approach to food. As I discussed in Part I, we as a society reject imperfect food so much so that it either rots in the fields or is left on shelves and eventually thrown out. Our search for physically perfect food, just as the Tomato Lady's search for the perfect tomato, has turned us into professional food-wasters.

In fact, many in today's society feel that they're doing themselves a disservice if they don't pick the best, i.e. the experiences or things that they think maximize happiness. This has led us to always look for the best available option or version of everything. Reinforcing this phenomenon is the relatively new and popular term:

FOMO

| fōmō |

noun

a state of mental or emotional strain caused by the fear of missing out.

It's a sensation that, for example, drives some of my generation to desperately text their friends and acquaintances, to find the most and the best immediately satisfying experience available at any given time. It was that same sensation that appears to have driven the Tomato Lady to search for the 'best' tomatoes. Without these, her sauce would not, in her mind, have provided the ultimate satisfactory experience.

Our generation, like the Tomato Lady, is far too picky about the physical attributes of the fruits and vegetables we buy. As I explained in Part I, if they don't look the way we think they should, if they have a small blemish, are 'ugly' or just not the 'right' size, we reject them.* This is part of the reason why 52% of all produce* is never eaten but instead rots in landfills, according to a 2011 Food and Agriculture Organization (FAO) Report. [Percentages calculated collectively for USA, Canada, Australia, and New Zealand].

My mom had another good story to tell and this one was about a concept she referred to as 'job lots,' or more colloquially, the 'reject pile.' 'Job lots' was a term grocers used to define goods that, at some point in their lifetime, drew the short straw or were about to do so. The term includes, for example:

- Boxes of goods with ripped or damaged labels;
- Produce that was getting close to its 'best by' date; or
- Dented cans.

My Nonno and Nonna on my mother's side saw value in these items, where others did not. They would buy crates, cartons and boxes of such 'job lots' wholesale and sell the physically 'imperfect' food to willing customers. Although my parents grew up (slightly) better off than my sour-milk-drinking great-grandfather, as immigrants fleeing postwar poverty in southern Italy they were far from affluent. Their customer base was of the same variety. Many had also grown

---

* We even reject canned food if the label is ripped or there is a dent in the can. More on this to come.

up poor, were living off of modest incomes, and appreciated a good deal when they saw one. Getting boxes of cereal with a damaged label at half the price was a good deal. Buying produce cheaper, just because it was approaching its best by date also made sense to them because they knew—from prior experience—that it could be prepared, canned and frozen. So, not only did my parents see the value of and 'in' these goods, so did their customers.

One particular job lot story my mom recounted really stuck with me.

"One summer it was so hot," she said, "that wholesalers could not keep strawberries cool enough. They were already beginning to go bad when my grandparents arrived to pick up their weekly food order. Knowing that my parents were resourceful (and also because they were running out of options), the manager pointed to a long wall of strawberries and said to them, 'You can have the entire wall from here to here—each pallet for $20 bucks…Oh screw it, you can have the whole wall for $100 bucks. I just want them out of here!' My parents ended up buying them all."

My mom continued. "My mother, my siblings and I spent the next two hours sorting, carving and repackaging them. There were boxes of ripe, but good whole strawberries and they were placed on sale for one discounted price. Those that were bruised were cut to remove the blemishes (in a manner that would have made Mr. Poitier proud) and packaged for a really deep discounted price. They obviously weren't your perfect Driscoll's berry but, believe it or not, there were buyers for both."

"That sounds like so much work," I commented. "How could they still make a profit?"

"Well," my mother explained without missing a beat, "my sisters and I were free labor. But even if you consider labor costs, given the price they paid for the whole wall, there was still a very good margin in it for them, a better one than for perfect produce, believe it or not. Some customers even bought two or three palettes and performed the labor of removing the blemishes themselves. That's how my parents became the outlet for job lot goods."

"The thought of selling cut-up strawberries in cartons is kind of sad though," I said, sighing.

But my mother reassured me. "No, there's nothing sad about it. In fact, I still remember the smile on my mother's—your grandmother's—face when the boxes sold like hotcakes. Not only did it make good business sense, but also, people who could not afford pricey strawberries suddenly could and, if that were not enough, my parents were preventing food waste, a concept near and dear to their hearts given how they grew up.

Their approach is in fact an example of the famous immigrant entrepreneurial spirit. This kind of attitude, seeing opportunity where others do not, is behind many of America's greatest inventions. In fact, today there are a number of businesses that have been born out of eliminating food waste, Adrian." (She was right, but you'll have to wait for Part III for that.)

"What else did they buy?" I asked.

"Lots of banged up cans. If not handled carefully, cans dent easily and people don't buy dented cans because they think something is wrong with the contents. But our customers, mostly immigrants who have seen worse, or the people in the area who did not have much money, didn't care. They knew the contents were good to eat."

At this point in the conversation, the entrepreneur in me was thinking of my grandparents in a much different manner. On one hand, they were savvy business people, intent on making a buck, and on the other they were compassionate and caring. I was impressed about both. On the latter, they were not only providing healthy, affordable food to an underserved population but also keeping imperfect, but good, food out of landfills. When I think of today's wave of new food-waste-fighting businesses (Part III), my grandparents were ahead of their time!

I loved hearing the stories almost as much, if not more, as my mother enjoyed telling them to me. And just when I thought it could not get better, she said, "Let's call my dad!" *

I was taken aback by her enthusiasm, but, of course, agreed. After all, how could I say no to such entertaining research? It sure beat the studying I'd come to the library to do. It was as if I was on a carnival ride, complete with surprising twists and turns; I simply was not ready to get off just yet. It was time to phone in the man himself. My grandpa, my *Nonno.*†

"Hold on," she said as she tried to patch him into our call. My mother is technologically challenged on a good day, so I took a seat, knowing this was going to take more than one attempt. Finally, I heard his signature voice.

"Eheeeelllloooo?" This dragged-out greeting was instantly recognizable as my grandpa's melodic Italian-English.

"Hi *Nonno!*"

"Ciao Bello! Eh-how you doin'?" he asked.

---

* My grandmother, the other half of Albo's Meats and Groceries, sadly died just before I was born.

† Even though my Nonno has a name—Franco Paulo—everyone, whether related or not, just calls him Nonno.

"Lots of work but I'm good! And you?"

"Me? I'm-a okay."

(My grandfather used the term 'okay' to mean anything ranging from 'good' to 'I've seen better days' but he was always steady as a rock, both in stature and in demeanor. I think he said 'okay,' rain or shine, because he had experienced much worse. He was one of those people my Aunt Ida referred to as having "gone without." I, on the other hand, had experienced far fewer hardships so okay still only meant *okay*.)

I started to tell him about my book, but my mom quickly took over. She had a way of explaining things to him more easily than I could.

"Papa, I was telling Adrian how you used to buy job lot goods and sell them at a discounted price to the customers who came to your store."

"Not just-a to 'dem,' my *Nonno* interrupted, "we also sold to da restaurants. Sometimes it was not even job lot. Just the outer box, the carton dey put the cans or boxes in, was damaged but everything inside was just-a fine." He paused briefly. "Da wholesaler couldn't sell these to da big stores—they were too picky. It also cost too much to return, so dey sold to us instead of throwing dem away."

So, I learned, not only was my grandfather selling job lot goods via retail, but also commercially. He had become a middleman, acting like an air traffic controller for *seemingly unsaleable* food. Some was sold normally, some at a discount to retail customers and some in bulk to restaurants. He was directing the supply safely from its source to people's tables, or otherwise to their stomachs and steering it clear from landfills.

Boy was I proud!

"Da pizza places were my biggest customers, Adrian," he said, "you met-a Mario Pizza." There he was again, referring to someone by what they did, just like the Tomato Lady. I had met Mario Pizza, a short man with a personality as fiery as his ovens. "Mario Pizza was one of my biggest customers. If I had-a job lot mushrooms, his pizza special would be with da mushrooms. If I had job lot peppers, his pasta special would have-a peppers. You get it? We both made money and da food did not go to da garbage."

"That's such a great story, Nonno."

"Eh—jaa! But eventually da wholesaler no wanna sell to us no more," my grandpa grumbled into his flip phone.

"What? Why?"

"Oh right! That's true!" My mom took over the explanation. "At one point the wholesalers were forced by the big box stores to stop selling to us and to throw the stuff away instead. Believe it or not, my parent's small store became too much of a competition on certain products, beating the superstores on price so they shut this business down. This is the not-so-bright side of commerce, particularly if you are a small, privately owned operation."

"*Nonno*," I interjected, "My mom also told me about the immigrant families who would come into the store at the end of the week to buy the stuff that was going bad. Is that true?"

"Yes, dey were regulars, came every Saturday afternoon to buy what did not sell." *Nonno* went on to explain that there was no shame in that. These were savvy shoppers and they had families to feed with not much money in their pockets. He was happy that they took the leftover food off his hands. "Dey look at wilted lettuce," he said, "offered me a price, and ate it that night. Dey bought almost 'expired' eggs and baked breads, and dey took all of the 'ugly' produce left over in my coolers, as well. Dey still saw value in it. Dey knew from experience that it was all safe to eat and dey picked it all up for a low price."

"I don't see that when I go to Whole Foods," my mom interjected.

"And what they no buy, eh, we eat!" *Nonno* chimed in, completing the story.

My mother's assertion that she had lived off of leftover groceries from the store was now officially confirmed. What others didn't want, kept their family of six happy and healthy.

"It sounds like you did not have a regular meal plan," I said. "You must have eaten so many different things then, no?" I was curious.

"Dat is right," said *Nonno*. "We wouldn't know what we put on da table until da end of da week."

My mom interrupted, "my mother, your grandmother, could transform anything into something delicious. Tomatoes became sauce, wilted veggies became soup, scarred but ripe eggplants were pickled. And that would feed our family for the rest of the week and sometimes months."

The two of them were now playing ping-pong with the stories.

"And some a-times, when we had a lot of leftovers, my wife, your *Nonna*, would cook it at the store. You could smell it from da street. People would come in and she would share what she made with dem."

"What did she make, *Nonno*?" I asked, secretly hoping the stories would never end.

"Oh you know. Good stuff like Pasta e fazul!" Officially known as Pasta e Fagioli (Pasta and Beans), it was a typical Neapolitan dish. Like many other dishes of that era, such as Pizza and Polenta, it falls under the umbrella of peasant food, *Cucina Povera,* as it was made with very inexpensive ingredients, creatively and deliciously assembled by the less well-to-do of Southern Italy. "Some people would take a break from da shopping to eat it and some would conveniently have da Tupperware and so they could take some home."

"*Nonno,* I learned about your father-in-law from my mom. Was your father involved in the business? Did he give you advice?" I asked.

"Ya even though he lived in Italia," *Nonno* said. "Once I told-a him that when I had a too much leftover food, I used to a-give it away to da people. He understood why because we grew up very poor and would have appreciated free food. But, one day he told-a me to throw it in da garbedge instead."

"WHAT?!" I blurted out, completely surprised after all I'd heard. "Why would he tell you to do that?" My mom, who had asked the same question years ago, knew the answer and provided it.

"Your great-grandfather felt that your grandfather was risking losing business by giving out free food. His logic was that, given his customer base, not only would they stop buying at full price if they knew they could just get a discount at the end of the week, but also, they might just all show up at the last minute and hope to get it for free."

The answer crushed an over-simplified belief I'd held, namely that those who threw out food, instead of donating it, were just 'bad' people. And after all of the inspirational stories I had heard about my family, I was disappointed that my great-grandpa didn't fulfill my naïve image of the food waste hero I had thought he was, the one that wasted nothing. Thinking back on this story after having learned more about the topics of donations and discounts, I recognize that business interests can sometimes conflict with social ones. In other words, there are 'bottom line' consequences to donating or discounting food that can put a retailer in a tough spot. I am a perfect example of what can happen: If there is nothing in the 'Seconds' box at the Twin Springs Fruit Farm's stand, I don't buy anything from them at all; it's just too expensive for me. I walk out empty-handed and the retailer lost a sale. My grandfather interrupted my thoughts.

"Okay Adriano, I got-a go. I wish you well with your book!"

I knew it was the end of this 'interview' for *Nonno*. My

grandpa, normally a man of very few words and little tolerance for boredom, had reached his limit on both fronts. I thanked him for sharing his precious stories and he hung up saying, "Ciao, Bello!" as he always does.

By the time I was done with this conversation, the library was closing, I had learned a great deal about the history of food waste in my family. In fact, I had learned that my grandparents, like my great-grandparents, were great Food Waste Warriors (FWWs). Of course they weren't perfect. Even though they bought 'job lots,' they still 'culled' the produce displays to make them look beautiful and attractive to customers; sometimes even threw things out, even though plenty of people would have come by to take the stuff off their hands. Sometimes, they simply did not have the time and the energy to call around and wait. However, despite their personal food-waste imperfections, they were far less wasteful on a bad day, than most of my generation is today.

FAMILY FWWS—THE LAST GENERATION?

Although I had to head home, the journey down memory lane of FWWs in my family had not ended just yet. There was one more family member I had to interview and that was my uncle, my mother's much younger brother. Both my mother and my aunt had suggested that he be the next person

I interview and so I did. I called Frank Albo Jr., the son of Nonno (Frank Albo Sr)

I had already heard many a tale about my uncle and his adventurous early years. He went from high school dropout to PhD recipient at Cambridge University and from gambler to bestselling writer. The period that I wanted to speak to him about, however, was when he was a salesman, namely a salesman of "distressed goods."

To understand this term, imagine a Campbell's Soup truck filled to capacity on its way to making a delivery to Target. The driver's quick pit stop at the bar the night before unfortunately lasted a little longer than originally planned, and it soon becomes late morning. En route to the store later that day, the back door pops open and the cargo spills out onto the road, knocking around and denting all the cans inside. These pallets of cans are now called distressed goods. But what happens to them?

Campbell's can't sell these anymore as they have been damaged (but the company doesn't care because it is insured). Target will not accept delivery because, to the store, the cans are worth as much as a tomato with a hole in it. Distressed goods were simply another version of the 'job lots' my grandparents used to buy and sell at their store. And when my uncle, the next generation, was in the business, the distressed goods often ended up in his hands. He in turn would sell the goods in bulk to nursing homes, schools or anyone who would have them. Distressed goods were a broader category than that of 'job lots' though, because it included anything and everything from toys to canned or boxed food, that had been scuffed up, bruised, or otherwise cosmetically damaged. The category did not, however, include fresh goods.

If you're like me, you've likely never heard of this underground economy before. That said, you've probably bought distressed products, for example at your local dollar store. I learned about this economy from my uncle, who was seemingly the last of the generation of food waste warriors in my family tree—until I joined that is! Unlike the more noble motivations of my grandparents, it was my young uncle's itchy palm that had attracted him to distressed goods. He, like many others today, saw the financial opportunities in selling products that would otherwise be tossed into the trash.

My mom was my connection to this lineage of FWW; her affinity for the subject, however, was weak at best, at least until I started working on converting her. As an executive at a large corporation, she eats out regularly and I can assure you, she is not walking out of those business dinners with a doggy bag.

On the other hand, she has grown increasingly excited about

my passion to reduce food waste. In fact, our conversations about the topic and about my experiences eventually caused her to 'carry the baton' herself and embrace her own roots all over again. One final story about my family will explain what I mean by this.

My mother had been on assignment in Europe, living alone in an apartment in Munich for over a year. This was enough time to accumulate lots of stuff, including food. In her last weeks there she called me, proudly announcing two accomplishments: "First," she said, "I just spent a weekend with *Opa*." *Opa* is my father's father who lives in Cologne. "You will be happy to know that I made (and froze) a large quantity of banana bread using his just about 'overdue eggs' and bananas that had gone black." She paused to receive my congratulations. "And now my second accomplishment," she continued, "my grocery embargo was a big success."

I needed a bit more of an explanation so my mother shared that she had decided a couple of weeks back to stop grocery shopping and simply live off of the remaining food supplies in her fridge and in her kitchen. She not only survived, but also managed to eat tasty, creative meals and invite guests! When it was time to leave, she gave away everything she had left on the shelves, including half bottles of spices and loose bags of tea, to her friends. I could practically see her smile through the telephone line!

Now back home in Princeton, she continues down her own food-waste conscious path. For example, instead of composting kale stems, she now cuts them up into small pieces and cooks them separately, letting them slowly soften as they sizzle in olive oil, just as I taught her. She even eats the onion from Marcella Hazan's tomato sauce! She may slip up from time to time, but she is much further down the path of honoring her food waste warrior lineage than she was in the past and this, she says, is thanks to me.

CHAPTER 11

POWER OF HABIT

———

My trip down memory lane not only provided great enlightenment but also ended up inspiring both me and in turn my mother. I was happy to have been the source of that inspiration, but for me, it was not enough. If I was going to go beyond inspiring, then I had to become a teacher. But to teach, I first had a lot more to learn. Most importantly, I had to learn how to change my behavior for good, not just until I met the next bruised peach.

This determination led me to research the topic of habits. After all the stories, I realized that my grandparents and great-grandparents simply had better food waste habits—ways of dealing with food—than the 90% of us today who throw food out too soon.

My research on habits took me straight to Charles Duhigg, an expert on the topic.

According to Duhigg, habits are actions people decide to do deliberately, at first, and then keep doing subconsciously, without focus and frequently. People can change their habits if they understand how habits operate. According to Duhigg, habits consist of a loop, which has three stages: a cue, which sets off a subconscious craving, a routine and a reward. The cue puts the brain on automatic pilot setting off a routine to receive a reward. When the cue and the reward connect, the brain develops a habit, which repeats itself.

Duhigg makes the point by describing his own habit, which essentially involved eating a cookie every day. He would get bored or hungry (the cue), automatically get up and go to the cafeteria and buy a cookie (routine) and have a break, a temporary distraction or a yummy treat (the reward). This habit, however, was not a good one as it caused him to gain weight, 8 pounds to be exact.

Fortunately, according to Duhigg, habits can be broken, if you take the time to understand them—to dissect and understand the components of the loop. Once you understand these, namely what cue (or trigger) sets the loop off, and what desire you are trying to satisfy (your reward), you can change the routine, breaking your bad habit and perhaps even creating a new, better one.

In the case of Duhigg's habit of going to eat a chocolate chip cookie every day, this could be changed as follows: feel boredom (the cue), get up and go for a walk outside (the new routine) and feel regenerated (the reward). This new habit is a good one that could also cause weight loss. In Duhigg's world, it is about recognizing the cue, changing the routine, and still getting a reward.

Unfortunately, while possible, breaking a habit is not necessarily easy. Believe me, I have tried to change several bad habits in the past with no success.

Judson Brewer offered me a relatable recipe for success in his short Ted Talk. Brewer is a psychiatrist and addiction expert, specifically in the field of habit change. For the past 20 years, and now at UMass Medical School and MIT, he has researched mindfulness techniques that effectively help quell cravings of all kinds. Brewer starts out his talk by explaining habits with the same "loop" Duhigg does—trigger (or cue), behavior (or routine), and reward. His advice, however, is to insert curiosity or mindfulness into the process. To make his point, he describes the results he achieved with smokers who were trying to break the habit of smoking.

The habit loop the smoker was following was this one: feel boredom or stress → smoke a cigarette → feel better. Unlike Duhigg, he did not ask the smoker to change the routine by not smoking. Rather, he asked the smoker to try to understand what he or she was feeling while he or she smoked, in order to insert curiosity and mindfulness into the process. Interestingly, one smoker he tested with this approach described her "mindful" smoking as follows: "Mindful smoking smells like stinky cheese and tastes like chemicals," or as Brewer summarized, "It tastes like shit." This 'aha!' moment allowed the smoker, and others he tested, to break the habit. His suggestion is therefore to notice the urge, get mindful or curious, then experience the joy of letting go of your normal routine. Brewer says this allows you to go from knowing in your head that what you are doing is a bad habit to knowing or feeling it in your bones and then doing something about it.

Another expert on habits is Stephen Guise, who wrote a book called Mini Habits. Like Duhigg, Guise explains how people form habits by repeating behaviors over time. He introduces the concept of a mini habit to reach larger goals. A mini habit is the smallest possible iteration of a larger positive habit (such as one push up a day to eventually reach your workout goal). Mini habits are in fact 'too small to fail' because the amount of willpower you need to accomplish them is equally small. Gratification is immediate and you feel so good about this achievement that it motivates you to set your sights higher. According to Guise, while his approach does not work for breaking bad habits such as alcohol abuse, it does help with what he calls passive bad habits such as laziness and procrastination. As Guise explains, since habit-forming requires willpower, which is in limited supply in any human being, focusing on changes that require only a little bit of willpower makes them happen quickly, leaving you enough to make bigger changes. Mini habits break goals into manageable steps that don't result in big disappointments. All in all, Guise works on the assumption that you are better off taking a small step (which is easy) than none at all and that, once mastered, small steps lead to big ones becoming easier to take. Guise even provides an eight-step approach (which incorporates Duhigg's habit loop).

That brings me back to Duhigg and another interesting thing I learned from him: habits are not only relevant for individuals, but also for corporate and other organizations. Alcoholics Anonymous (AA) is a perfect example. Duhigg explains how this organization taps into the habit loop to better achieve its goals. Focusing on the loop, AA tries to shift the routine once someone gets the cue for drinking. AA replaces the routine of drinking with the routine of companionship. AA teaches individuals to examine their cravings closely to find out what drives them, and then introduces both a spiritual element as well as one of community to help them change their ways.

Other organizations or corporations take a look at their 'organizational habits'—habits that are necessary to keep firms functioning—and see how these can be improved with the benefit of the habit loop. For example, in the area of work safety, the goal can be to create new and better organizational habits. Others have even identified certain 'keystone habits' that, if changed, can have a domino effect, cascading through the firm and forcing change in other seemingly unrelated areas, thus unlocking further benefits.

LESSONS LEARNED

Looking into the past often helps us to better understand the present. Understanding how we got where we are, allows us to see if this where we want to be, or how we want to be doing things.

My quest to better understand my family's food waste history started off with a lot of questions. It involved learning from my experiences of those of others. I learned that many of the forgotten habits, actions, and attitudes of my ancestors are instrumental tools in the fight against food waste and that Americans' current detrimental food waste habits can be changed for the better. I also learned that eliminating food waste can not only help individuals and the environment, but also corporations both young and old.

In Part III, I will look at some companies have tried changing their food waste habits for the better and their experiences with the endeavor, some good and some bad. I will also identify certain startups that are employing good food waste habits from the outset and profiting from their unique positioning. But first, I will look at how I improved my own food waste habits and provide a few simple tips for how you can improve yours.

PART 3

THE FOOD WASTE OPPORTUNITY

CHAPTER 12

INDIVIDUAL INITIATIVES

——

THE FOOD WASTE OPPORTUNITY—ALL ABOARD

The food waste problem is clearly bad and, unfortunately, getting worse. The good news is, something can be done about it. Individuals, governments, NGOs and corporations, both old and new, all have roles to play. The potential impact of getting involved and collaborating is immensely beneficial and addresses the social, economic and environmental issues of food waste. Some have even capitalized on the food waste problem to launch new and exciting business ventures.

CREATING A HABIT OF FOOD CONSERVATION: PERSONAL LESSONS LEARNED

JUST LIKE EVERYONE ELSE

So as you've learned, I started out no different than anyone else. Before this journey, I too contributed my personal 300-pound bag share of edible garbage to the 40% of food that is wasted every year. I too had very bad food waste habits. For example:

- When I was hungry or bored, or just needed to satisfy a culinary interest (cue), I'd walk into a store, fascinated by all the options and buy more than I needed (routine). Once back home, I'd toss out the old, replenish my supplies with a fresh selection and satisfy my taste buds (reward);

- When I was hungry, bored, read a new rave review on Eater.com or just wanted to treat myself (cue), I'd go to a restaurant and, fascinated by all the options and choices, order more than I could eat (routine), thereby satisfying my taste buds and penchant for novelty (reward), but would not take home the leftovers;

- When I wanted a distraction or felt it was time to clean up or de-clutter (cue), I'd go to my fridge or my shelves and toss out anything that I considered old (routine) and have space again for new stuff (reward).

The examples go on and on, but you get the point. Some of you probably have the same habits.

Fortunately for me, at one point, I also got curious, just as Brewer suggests. It started with my 'mindful moment' with the onion—should I eat it instead of tossing it out? It continued after my one-pot meal when I developed a fascination with my family history—its relation to food and food waste as compared with mine. I also took a few pointers from a pile of green beans. Intuitively, I started changing habits one small step at a time, like taking leftovers home after a restaurant meal and actually eating them, for example. Unfortunately, my slip-up on the organic farm—and this right after witnessing food waste (in the pizza business) in a way I had never seen before—told me I needed to better understand habits and how to change them. I needed to develop a system to change them for good. And now that I have, I want to share a couple of personally developed tips with you.

ME AFTER ME—FOOD WASTE PREVENTION HABITS FOR ALL TO ENJOY

The following lessons were developed over time, and while difficult at first, adhering to them now comes naturally to me. Like me, you can start with one; the rest may come naturally. No matter what, you will increase your food-telligence along the way:

- You can make delicious salsa, or tomato sauce, with ugly tomatoes (butter and an onion—check out Marcella Hazan's recipe), so don't ignore them, throw them out or poke holes in them during the purchasing process—the Tomato Lady had it all wrong. Also, canned or frozen properly, the sauce can be stored safely for months.

- On a similar note, if a fruit or vegetable has lost its luster, or has a bruise, not only can you remove the 'blem'—recall Mr. Poitier—but also you won't notice this in a pie or a soup. Wilted greens are a great example. Limp kale makes for a sad salad, but it will still be delicious when cooked, in a frittata for example.

- Start composting! All it takes is an Internet search or a few phone calls to see what your municipality or region has on offer. I *even* found a way at Georgetown. (It requires biking thin green bags of food scraps to my local farmers market, but I get fresh air in the process. And if you are wondering why this is such an accomplishment, read on).

- Look or ask for 'seconds,' 'culls,' 'misfits,' or discounted items at your favorite farmers market or your (progressive) grocery store. They might look a bit weird or off, or have a shorter shelf life, but they'll taste just as good as the pretty variety and cost you less money.

- On that note, check out 'ugly' food distributors such as Imperfect Produce (if you are on the West Coast) and Hungry Harvest (if you are on the East Coast). I've been a happy customer of the latter for months now. Both are delivery services working to reduce waste by creating demand and accessibility for recovered groceries. You'll get healthy food, great value and a guilt-free conscience knowing you're saving food from landfills!

- Take home your restaurant leftovers, and—wait for it—eat them. The same goes for leftovers from school or office events. Food in the trash = an unhappy planet!

- Before you go shopping, look at what you have at home. You can live off of things in your fridge or on your shelf for longer than you think you can—just ask my mom.

- Don't buy more than you can eat—even if it is on sale! But, if you do, invite friends over, and cook or store the food for later enjoyment.

- Dedicate a corner of your fridge as the "Eat me first" zone. Regularly check the condition of the items in your fridge to see how soon they might spoil and place it in this zone. And stick to it! Bon àppetit!

- If you are going on vacation or a longer trip, gift a friend, neighbor or roommate with any food that might go bad during this time. Or check out the OLIO app, a platform that connects neighbors with each other and with local shops so surplus food and other items can be shared, not thrown away.

- On the flipside, there is no shame in accepting food that might otherwise go to waste from others. I regularly do this when friends or co-workers go out of town and save quite of a bit on my weekly grocery bill as a result.

- In this context, be wary of "best by" dates. Test the food before you toss it, or freeze it for later use. An egg past its best by date is still perfectly fine as long as it doesn't float when submerged in water, for example.

- Check out smaller produce stores in the area, primarily at the end of the week—you might be able to pick up things more cheaply. Also, once the shopkeepers get to know you, they might even call you and put things aside before they toss them out. You'll quickly discover that they're all food-waste warriors at heart too. ;)

- Learn about product storage techniques that make food last longer. Just ask Alexa. Or Google. I, for example, freeze fresh herbs if I know I can't use them on time and use them in a soup later. I also freeze overripe fruit like strawberries and bananas and make amazing smoothies!

- Finally, make your own one-pot meal one day, have a mindful moment, and think of what else you can add to this list or make it your own! If you'd like, please share your ideas with me on Twitter @adrian_hertel. I'd love to hear them!

While developing these new habits, I had to draw a few lines in the sand, particularly where my personal commitment to preventing food waste started interfering with my health or my responsibilities. So now:

- I refuse to personally eat leftover or rescued junk food. (I do, however, happily share it with my roommate, who already subsists mostly on Kit-Kats, Pop-Tarts and pound cake);

- I don't force myself to eat everything before it goes to waste. This quickly led me to gain weight, just as it did Dana Gunders, who gained 10 pounds when her commitment compelled her to eat *all* the leftovers at company events *all* the time; and

- I no longer try to rescue all the food I come across. Living on a college campus where surplus food is left out by shops and events on a daily basis, this task quickly proved herculean and time-consuming and caused me to fall behind with other responsibilities. (I do, however, still advertise these leftovers to hungry Georgetown students on my Twitter).

FURTHER INSPIRATION

If the above is not enough inspiration or advice for how to change your personal food waste habits and make your individual contribution to the cause, you can also google "Save Food from the Fridge," which provides added tips to keeping food fresher longer, or "29 Smart and Easy Tips to Reduce Food Waste" on greatest.com. I was happy to see that the latter article references a lot of my 'hard-learned new habits' and categorizes tips by what you can do at the store, at home, and during meals.

BENEFITS

In the end, you will see that individual changes have benefits. Changing my food habits and adhering to new ones not only helps me save money and reduce my negative environmental footprint, but also frees up time and makes me feel like a better person.

CHAPTER 13

GOVERNMENT & NGO: INITIATIVES AND BENEFITS

———

Governments and NGOs also have a role to play in the fight against food waste. They have long led the way in increasing national *food-telligence,* as it relates to nutrition for example. Another aspect of *food-telligence* in which they have the potential to make a great impact is in preventing food waste.

GOVERNMENT INITIATIVES IN AMERICA

One of the hidden champions in the war against food waste is the US Environmental Protection Agency (EPA). It has created a document, the Food Recovery Hierarchy, that is at the core of many public and private efforts to curb food waste. Reminiscent in spirit to the household phrase "Reduce-Reuse-Recycle," it looks like this:

The upside-down pyramid ranks, from most to least preferred, the six ways of dealing with unwanted or unsold food, some of which are discussed below. The goal is to make this chart as well-known as the food pyramid and, more so, to encourage both individuals and businesses to act on it.

The document has already had a great influence in three principal areas—source reduction, redirection and recycling—all of which are components of the pyramid.

Source reduction: The best way to reduce food waste, is also the most obvious one: source reduction. Simply put: you don't have to get rid of waste you do not produce in the first place. The concept is both socially positive and makes financial sense. One example of source reduction is the following: Inspired by the Food Recovery Hierarchy, one frozen pie company reduced the amount of dough to be trimmed off of its pies before freezing and selling them. This small efficiency saved them 300 tons of wasted pie dough a year. Similarly, General Mills changed the way that it heated cheese on its frozen pizza in the preparation phase. This innovation allowed more of the toppings to stick to the pizza and, as a result, less to find their way onto the floor and into the garbage. These small improvements, inspired by a simple ranking, had big social and economic impact.

Redirection: The second-best use for uneaten food is redirecting it to feed people—Option #2 in the Food Recovery Hierarchy. More and more players in the food industry are now sending unused food and ingredients to food banks or other food organizations to feed people in need. See below for more on this.

Recycling: Since not all food waste can be avoided and not all food can be redirected, there is also a third initiative that is being used to address unavoidable food waste. This method, also referred to in the above diagram, essentially involves recycling. Such waste is being incorporated into animal feed, turned into compost or used to create energy through anaerobic digestion.

GOVERNMENT INITIATIVES OUTSIDE OF AMERICA

Governments around the world are jumping on the food waste reduction bandwagon, as well. Take Italy for example. Legislators there have introduced financial incentives, i.e. tax breaks, to companies that reduce the amount of food they waste. France has gone the other way, essentially banning food waste by introducing fines, for example, for supermarkets that throw away food that is edible or can be used in animal feed. Fines range from single to double-digit thousands of Euros, and some offenses even result in jail time for responsible individuals.

The following statistic explains why many European governments are taking the food waste problem so seriously: the 88 million tons of waste Europe currently produces is expected to grow to 120 million tons by 2020! But not if drastic measures are taken first.

LOCAL GOVERNMENT INITIATIVES

Local governments are also doing their part to fight food waste. Many municipalities, including my hometown of Princeton, have introduced curbside organic pickup to keep food out of landfills. This convenience encourages consumers, the biggest wasters in the food chain, to do their part.

Other local regulators have started initiatives favoring composting and some are even creating composting facilities. Government bodies both in the US and elsewhere around the world, are encouraging the production of anaerobic digestion plants. Anaerobic digestion is a process taking place within closed facilities that safely converts solid waste, be it sewage or food scraps, into electricity. As our supply of fossil fuels continues to diminish, technology such as this is expected to play an increasingly important role in the fight against food waste and for sustainability in general.

NON-GOVERNMENTAL INITIATIVES

FOOD WASTE ALLIANCE

A number of non-governmental agencies and associations are also taking the initiative to reduce the food waste problem. One of the most important ones in my view is the Food Waste Alliance (FWA), an alliance of three major industries that are large contributors to food waste, namely food and beverage manufacturers, food and beverage retailers, and the food service industry (i.e. restaurants).

The FWA was formed in 2011 with three main goals in mind:

- To decrease food waste generation;
- To increase the amount of food donated; and
- To increase recycling of food waste.

Remind you of anything? Yes, the FWA is a collaborative effort to support the initiatives outlined in the Food Recovery Hierarchy, again illustrating the great impact that governmental bodies can have.

The following statistics highlight why the efforts of FWA are so important:

- 84.3% of unused food in restaurants goes to waste;
- 14.3% is recycled; and only
- 1.4% gets donated.

By sharing best practices and ideas, those involved in the food industry can fight this growing problem, respect government goals and objectives, help those in need, and also increase their bottom line.

CHAMPIONS 12.3

On the topic of the bottom line, allow me to introduce David Lewis, the CEO Of Tesco, an international grocery store chain, and also the Chairman of *Champions 12.3*. *Champions 12.3* is a group of 40 public and private sector leaders committed to reducing food waste by advancing the UN Sustainable Development Goal 12.3: to halve food waste per capita by 2030 and reduce food waste worldwide.

According to Lewis, "There are still too many inside business and government who are unaware or unsure of the impact they can have by reducing waste, and who are not doing enough to help tackle it." This problem is due in part to the fact that there is not enough published economic analyses to demonstrate the financial gains made in reducing food waste. Champions 12.3 recognized that they had to provide this economic data to support what everyone knows intuitively, namely that "waste is a drain on money and resources."

Champions 12.3 commissioned a report from the Waste & Resources Action Programme (WRAP), which sets out "the clear investment case for reducing food waste," a case that few CEOs are aware of. After collectively analyzing more than 1,200 business sites of more than 700 companies in 17 countries and in various sectors ranging from food retail to food and hospitality services, the report found that "on average, for every $1 a company invested in food loss and waste reduction—through training programs, providing equipment like scales to quantify food, and improving storage and packaging—they received a $14 return on investment, with restaurants benefitting most." The report goes on to emphasize that this positive effect on the bottom line, together with non-financial strategic benefits, including better stakeholder relationships, makes the business-minded case for fighting food waste.

CHAPTER 14

CORPORATE INITIATIVES: INTERNATIONAL AND NATIONAL AND NONE

Who said you can't teach an old dog new tricks? More and more existing businesses and organizations, whether international, national or regional, are changing their bad food waste habits, albeit with varying degrees of success. Unfortunately, there are others that continue to turn a blind eye to the problem and deserve some prodding (not to mention a lesson or two from Duhigg). Those that take initiative see benefits, while those that don't, I predict, may eventually be left behind.

INTERNATIONAL STAR ON THE BLOCK

SODEXO

Sodexo, the second largest food service business in the world, is one of the biggest stars in food waste prevention that I encountered in the course of my research, and is definitely food-telligent. It takes food waste seriously, both internally in its operations and externally through its support of Campus Kitchens and The Food Recovery Network, two leading food recovery organizations. Sodexo's history even has a positive story to tell.

The company was founded in 1966 by Pierre Bellon in Marseilles, France and is now the worldwide leader of what it calls "quality of life services." These services include, amongst other things, providing corporate and government employees, students and faculty with good, nutritious meals.

I spoke to Nell Fry, Senior Manager of Sustainability Field Support at Sodexo. She described what Sodexo is doing to reduce food waste and the positive implications this has had for the organization. Fry chalks up the company's success in this regard to the fact that "[f]ood waste is a nexus issue for us. Addressing the problem impacts many other corporate social responsibility and sustainability metrics we use to measure our performance. It is a priority for the CEO and, as a result, it is top of mind for the company."

While having top-down commitment is important, however, Fry said that 'buy-in' from staff, partners and other stakeholders also matters in order to ingrain good organizational food habits as a way of life. This is why Sodexo sponsors initiatives such as '#WasteLessWeek,' which has been going on for 20 years. With this initiative, the company educates its operators on all facets of waste, including food waste, raising consciousness about the topic and achieving reductions in food waste. Fry also attributes the broader 'buy-in' to the corporate culture and, more specifically, the French culture, which is socially minded and permeates Sodexo. Whatever it is, it appears to be working and Fry is proud to tell their story.

"By focusing on best-practice [and] sharing and participating in industry groups like the Food Waste Reduction Alliance," mentioned above, Sodexo has been able "to make an impact up and down the supply chain." The company educates its distributors about issues that are important to it and empowers its site operators with information they can use to craft creative solutions to problems like food waste, such as donating food. As a result, their customers not only commit to, but also contribute to and support Sodexo's zero waste goals.

While Sodexo is happy about the positive social impact it is having in various communities, Fry is quick to remind me that "the bottom line is key!" According to Fry, "you get better results when it's not only the right thing to do but also the best thing to do for your business." And fortunately, Sodexo was quick to realize that reducing food waste contributes to improving the bottom line, confirming the results of the WRAP report mentioned in Chapter 13.

Fry outlined how mindful Sodexo is about its role. As a caterer to many commercial operations, Fry described Sodexo as "a guest in our client's home." Sodexo runs the kitchens, makes the food, hires the people and, in the process, produces a lot of the emissions and waste. The company sees these as responsibilities to take seriously. "When we buy an apple," said Fry, "we want to use it. We don't want to compost it and we don't want to pay for something that is not consumed." This particularly matters given the amount of food that is being thrown out and the number of adults and children who are "food insecure." In other words, given this reality, Sodexo sees throwing food away not only as bad business, but also as inequitable.

While Fry explained how Sodexo offers a good corporate model for sustainability practices and preventing food waste, she also offered perspective on a personal level. Fry finds sustainability and fighting food waste in her personal life harder to practice than she does at work. She feels that the government can do much more, for example, by offering systematic incentives that encourage people to behave sustainably at home.

"We need experiences living in sustainable communities, learning about and seeing the dangers of landfills and how our individual actions are impacting the poorest people in our communities," she said. The fact that there are no consumer-level landfill bans and that individuals are not responsible for their own waste in the US is, according to Fry, also unhelpful.

Fry made the same observation I did, namely that embracing the issue is a matter of culture and habits, and that changing habits is not easy. According to Fry, it takes time to change habits, "especially around food, which is such an intimate part of your life," and also when there is no external motivation. The US is particularly lacking in this regard. In other parts of the world, notably Europe, one has to pay for the amount of garbage one produces. In the majority fo the US one does not, and so there is no incentive to reduce waste, at least not an incentive that affects one's wallet. That said, since food waste, once known, is an issue that can resonate with everyone, she is optimistic that progress can be made on the individual level. As a result, she sees embracing the reduction of food waste as both a corporate and individual opportunity that should not be passed up. This outlook makes Sodexo my international Food Waste Reduction Star.

NATIONAL/REGIONAL STARS

A number of smaller national or regional corporations also deserve a shout-out. I found two worthy of mention, even though they are not as advanced and all-embracing as Sodexo.

GEORGIA TECH

Georgia Institute of Technology, or Georgia Tech, is an institution that has taken food waste reduction seriously; in fact, for this institution (unlike others—see below), reducing food waste is a huge priority. The university food service operator reached its goal of having zero waste in 2015! In addition to that, a pre- and post-consumer composting system, which was introduced on campus, has reduced food waste by 98 percent for two of the university's residence halls, while generating fertilizer for a local farm. According to the Institute, the cost for implementing composting on campus was negligible.

RUNZA

Runza is a family-operated fast food restaurant with 84 locations. Despite the fact that it has so many locations, you have probably never heard of this small chain unless you're from Nebraska, where Runza is very well known for fresh fast food.

With their relatively small stores, mostly in towns of fewer than 10,000 people, the amount of waste doesn't really amount to much (at least compared to Sodexo or other fast food chains) but it does if you factor in all 84 locations. Yet, when I asked Donald Everett, CEO of Runza, "How do you manage food waste?" he simply answered, "We don't!" In reality, however, that was not the whole story.

An environmentally conscious man himself, Everett does make an effort. He recalled a time when recycling wasn't yet mainstream. He even noted that he was quick to join the early trials of municipal recycling programs at all the Runza locations, despite the added cost. Having created his own compost pile in his backyard, Everett was also eager to implement his own commercial composting solutions at Runza.

In 2014, Everett trialed composting at two Runza restaurants located in larger cities; those were the only ones with access to composting services. And, on the surface, the initiative seemed to be a success. The two Runza locations saw their trash pickups cut in half from four pickups per week to two. The employees embraced the extra effort required in separating their waste and were excited to be making their operations more sustainable. Everett added that it was especially the young generation that was open to spending more time and effort to contribute to "the greater good."

Unfortunately, however, Everett soon found that the "financials of composting" just didn't make sense. The savings from the decrease in trash pickups were minimal and, when combined with the additional cost of paying a third company for composting, the initiative actually led to a net loss of $190 a month per location. "That doesn't seem like a lot," said Everett, but "when you only have 2-3% margin, it gets eaten up pretty fast." According to Everett, businesses like Whole Foods, with much larger margins, could afford initiatives such as the one Everett implemented, but he simply could not justify the costs and thus discontinued the practice.

While Runza locations no longer compost, they do well on other food waste management endeavors. Unlike other fast food restaurants, cafeterias, buffets, and restaurants, at Runza little preparation is required. Everett prides himself on the fact that his fast food is made to order fresh. As a result, there are not many prepared foods and ingredients lying around that have to get thrown out at the end of the day. Additionally, unlike many restaurants that serve portions two to four times times the recommended amount, Runza offers portions that are just the right size, according to Everett (like the ones my great-grandparents prepared in their pot.) As a result, everything that is ordered is eaten.

Donating food to prevent food waste is, unfortunately, not an initiative Everett is willing to consider. Not only is it not an option for Runza, given its mostly rural locations, but Everett also had other reasons that made him uneasy about the idea. He mentioned one in particular. "As you might know, Chipotle's stock still hasn't recovered two years after its E. coli incident." Everett was implying that the public relations backlash would have been made even worse if this batch involved food donated to homeless people, who already suffer enough.

Despite his mixed experiences with food waste prevention initiatives, Everett does remain open to new ways of addressing the problem, even if not all of them work commercially. In fact, he is firmly of the view that food waste management and sustainability in general should be supported by government initiatives to facilitate eco-friendly behaviors. Like Fry, he seems to wish that the government did more to encourage and perhaps even enforce better food waste habits. Having understanding for the problem, implementing measures on his own to the extent feasible, and seeing how those measures engage his employees, Everett certainly sees the opportunities in this space. This is why Runza made my National/Regional Star list.

NO STARS AT ALL

Others unfortunately still do not recognize the value of what Fry and others do, and may be left behind. I was disheartened to learn that one organization that falls into that bucket, is my very own university, Georgetown.

THE CORP

An example of this at Georgetown is the Students of Georgetown Inc., otherwise known as "The Corp." The Corp runs food, beverage and other student services on campus and is deeply ingrained into campus culture and lifestyle, especially for staff and students. I interviewed three employees of the Corp who work in different functions and what I learned was both eye-opening and disappointing.

VITAL VITTLES

Marcos Morales is the director of Vital Vittles, which opened in 1973 as the first storefront of the then newly founded Students of Georgetown Inc. Vital Vittles started as a food co-op with a limited selection but has since grown into a full-service grocery store, carrying everything from frozen foods and cereals, to meats and vegetables. With its on-campus location, it offers great convenience to students and staff.

Morales talked to me about the amount of food spoilage he sees at Vital Vittles, particularly since they started selling prepared foods and fresh fruit. While the grocery operation tries to track sales and inventory through a point of sale system in an effort to control inventory and reduce waste, "reconciling what came in and when is manual and very cumbersome and error-prone," Morales said, adding, "It is difficult to determine ideal order quantities" for the numerous products they stock. This inefficiency unfortunately results in unwanted spoilage. According to Morales, during the semester, staff members are so busy with other things, they do not even have time to coordinate and contain spoilage. As a result, improving the tracking system and food waste prevention in general simply is not a priority. "On my list, it's at the bottom," Morales explained. This results in a particularly unwelcome situation at the end of each semester when students are forced to leave campus. At these times, the store has so much leftover produce and products, that it ends up throwing out most of the food on hand. According to Morales, this waste is a very large quantity.

I could not believe my ears when Morales explained this to me, so I decided to test the veracity of his story. This year, just before winter break started, I showed up at Vital Vittles to inspect the leftovers and see firsthand what was done with them. Morales was right! When the store closed for the holidays it was still relatively well stocked with a large amount of un-purchased perishable goods. These goods would have found their way straight to the garbage and eventually a landfill if I had not shown up. The following picture shows just how much food would have been discarded if I had not visited the store to collect 'my prize.'

Morales did not appear happy with the fact that a lot of the left-over food at Vital Vittles goes to waste, but at the same time he did not appear to make it a priority to change this, nor was he forced to by the University. Unlike my grandparents, he had no personal skin in the game. He did lament the fact that he does not have any composting possibilities and that donating the food is apparently "currently not a feasible solution". At the same time, however, Morales expressed a pessimistic economic view of undertaking such food waste prevention initiatives. In his view, the cost of labor associated with keeping goods from being tossed into the trash, outweighs the cost of spoilage.

I took issue with this point and introduced Morales to ReFed. ReFed is a collaboration of businesses, non-profits, foundations and government leaders that came together to analyze food waste problems and come up with practical solutions. It has come up with 27 of the most cost effective ways to decrease food waste based on socio economic value, business profit potential and other non financial impacts and has in fact developed an easy data-driven guide for businesses, government funders and non profits to collectively reduce food waste at scale. ReFed may be able to provided Morales with some necessary Food-telligence.

HILLTOSS

My second conversation was with Emily Leeser, director of another Corp location, The Hilltoss. Hilltoss provides healthy eating options on the south side of campus by serving mainly salads and other fresh treats. Leeser's experience also reminded me of that of my grandparents. According to Leeser, when the weekend approaches, most her supplies face spoilage. Unlike my grandparents, who were open on weekends and still had a chance to sell their perishables, albeit at reduced prices, or even to give the food away, Leeser is not allowed to. Not only are there rules that prevent her from donating the perishable items she has on hand to a homeless shelter, for example, but there are also rules, authored by the Department of Health, that mandate that unsold food cannot sit in the fridge for more than seven days. As a result, when the weekend approaches, all perishable items, such as chicken, avocados and lettuce, have to be thrown out. Leeser admitted that the amount of food spoilage is "not nice to witness," and that it also cuts into revenues.

Leeser thought about composting the leftover items, but this was not an easy solution—Georgetown provided no assistance. Leeser decided to take matters into her own hands by hiring a third-party composting company—which is commendable—but she was quick to highlight all of the negatives. Not only did contacting several third-party compost company, and eventually contracting just one involve a big "hullabaloo", as Leeser called it, but also training staff to compost is "anything but easy." She also discovered that the companies were either incredibly strict or unreliable—their most recent contractor just stopped making pickups one day, out of the blue. As a result, according to Georgia Reading, Sustainability Director at the Corp—see below—the composting initiative is not operating properly and is not a sustainable solution.

CORP DIRECTOR OF SUSTAINABILITY

This takes me to the topic of sustainability of the Corp in general and, more specifically, my conversation with Georgia Reading, the Corp's director of sustainability. Reading is personally committed to reducing food waste on campus, shown by her partnering with *Hoyas Rescuing Leftover Cuisine*. Logistics and liability issues, which are outside of the Corp's control, unfortunately are hampering her endeavors. An even bigger roadblock is, however, within the Corp's control. This involves a broader cultural commitment to combatting food waste from the top down, like the one that contributes to the success at Sodexo.

Let's start with logistics and legalities. According to Reading, these issues are particularly evident following parents' weekends and student welcome weekends, when there is always an abundance of leftover food. While the leftovers could theoretically be offered to homeless people, according to Reading, no one is willing to pick the food up. Additionally, organizing this project involves logistics that her understaffed office cannot handle and involves liabilities that the Corp does not want.

One thing that Reading is trying to address on campus is composting, but the experience has been frustrating given the lack of buy-in for the issue of food waste from the top. In fact, Reading feels she is getting "a false sense of support" for all her sustainability efforts. As a result, a lot of good initiatives simply "don't get off the ground because people spend too much time talking about the problem and not enough time doing anything about it."

This lack of commitment to reduce food waste results in lack of funding for such efforts as well. While trash pickup is included in the rent at Georgetown, compost pickup is not.

Since it is still a niche service, with no local providers, the cost involved is about $600 per month. Arranging composting for the entire Corp therefore would require an additional budget amount, and the fruits of Reading's efforts to secure some level of funding for her composting initiative have been very disheartening. In her view, those who hold the purse strings don't really care about sustainability or reducing food waste. "No one is going to do anything for the sake of the earth simply because it's good," she said. The cost involved is too big of a financial burden.

Reading is still trying hard to convert the detractors because "the Corp is determined to get on with the initiative of composting or rescuing food." In Reading's view this may, however, require a broader campus movement and more resources for the sustainability office, which currently only consists of herself, one other person and a couple of summer interns. It also would require the University to take a serious look in the mirror. Reading drew a comparison to other universities in the area such as George Washington University, Howard University and American University, all of which are composting. "We can't blame it on lack of resources, if other area universities found them and excelled."

To highlight the lack of top-down commitment to sustainability in general and to the food waste issue in particular at Georgetown, Reading points to the scant number of environmentally related courses offered at the university. Given the lack of prioritization of this issue from the top, sustainability issues in general are simply not on campus radar, and not part of campus culture. Reading referred to one recent and specific example of a campus dance group that tried selling reusable Corp cups: nobody bought them. "Contrast this to life at Middlebury," she said, "and you'd be shocked." When Reading was there for her senior year, she lived in a house that was fully self-sustaining! Spin classes were introduced that generated campus electricity. Unlike Middlebury, Georgetown does not appear to make sustainability a priority as 'they'd rather spend the money bringing Bill Clinton to campus."

Citing another example of the lack of food waste prevention culture, Reading pointed to Hilltoss. Although it is making an effort to compost, "no one goes there because they compost." Rather, patrons go because of the relatively low cost and convenience. Reading believes that this reality is a direct result of the fact that Georgetown does not foster a culture of sustainability, nor one of food waste prevention. According to Reading, the University does not encourage nor does force people to change their ways. This, according to Reading, is a lost opportunity not only for the University, but also for the Corp. In fact, in her view, given that the Corp is the largest nonprofit student-run business in the world, if it focused more on sustainability issues like food waste, it could create a real brand and be a real influencer. All in all, the lack of interest in the topic of sustainability and food waste has caused Reading to lose her passion for the role.

The Corp therefore is missing out on the many benefits associated with a commitment to preventing food waste, ranging from cost reduction to environmental improvement to social benefits. And, if Reading is any indication, it is also paying the price of employee frustration. This lack of interest in the topic of food waste cost the Corp its 'star' in my eyes.

CHAPTER 15

NEW KIDS ON THE BLOCK: THE FOOD WASTE OPPORTUNITY

Fortunately, organizations like Georgetown that do not appreciate the problems associated with food waste are decreasing in number. Not only that, but also an increasing number of parties are aware of the benefits of food waste prevention and are even reaping the benefits of solving the problem. In fact, a whole new breed of startups has jumped onto the food waste bandwagon in recent years, with innovative ways of addressing the problem, doing good and making money in the process.

ADRIAN'S TOP 5 LIST

A Google search including the terms "food waste startup" will turn up a number of lists of the Top 10 or Top 5 most impactful startups leaving their mark on the food waste problem. (I even found one outlining 59 Organizations Fighting Food Loss and Waste on Foodtank.com.) The search may also feature articles about startups that have achieved the most funding from venture capitalist or other investors. In one way or another, they address the items on the Food Waste Recovery pyramid.

Having researched this area extensively, as well as having performed a number of interviews, I decided to come up with my own list of 'Top Food Waste Start Ups.' Mine includes organizations both near and far, those employing old tricks and new technology, and one personal favorite, located around the corner.

AGRI GAIA SYSTEMS CO.

Let's start with one further from home: Agri Gaia Systems Co., Japan's largest animal feed maker. Agri made my Top 5 list for two reasons. First, it addresses a problem in a country, Japan, whose food industry is the biggest producer of food waste in the world. Second, I appreciated the story about how the company came about.

Starting with the story, Agri was founded by a former garbage truck driver Hiroyuki Yakou. Yakou became so fed up with dumping loads of discarded food every day, that he decided to do something about it: he started Agri. Whereas he used to cart truckloads of rice balls, sandwiches and milk into landfills on a daily basis, these leftovers are now brought to his factory on the outskirts of Tokyo, where the food scraps are turned into animal feed for pigs and chickens. Strict government legislation, which requires convenience stores and restaurants to throw out items at the end of the day, provide him with a constant flow of "free raw materials." Another law, which gradually increases recycling targets for companies that dispose of the vast quantities of food waste in Japan, and gives them more incentive to work with recycling companies, is an added boost to business. Add to this equation the fact that the price of imported animal feed has risen considerably, and you can see how Yakou's products (and those of other startups in the fledgling Japanese food recycling industry) are a real hit. Agri makes my Top 5 list not only because it makes both social and economic sense, but also because I like the rags to riches (or rather the trash to treasure) story.

DYNOS

Number two on my Top 5 list is Dynos, a technology company, which is leaving its mark in the food waste space by offering dynamic pricing capabilities to restaurants. Dynos was founded Sahaj Sharda, my peer and a sophomore Georgetown, (which is one reason that it made my top 5).

Dynos addresses two segments of the restaurant business. 1) It helps manage supply, 2) it stabilizes & increases demand. These two improve a business's overall efficiency and "efficiency is always better for the market," Sharda says.

According to Sharda, 12-16% of the average restaurant's inventory is thrown away—this is both "morally and financially bad."

Dynos attacks the problem of wasted food by allowing restaurants to make dynamic adjustments to prices. "This has a positive knock-on effect," says Sharda. It allows businesses to better manage what they have, what they do with what they have, and manage time and attention. Dynos showcases the importance of technology in the war against food waste, another reason it made my Top 5 list.

Dynamic pricing has a very large potential for businesses of all sizes. Fiola Mare is one of D.C.'s finest seafood restaurants, but during the day it is often empty. Students in the area are a potential market, but the restaurant's prices make it inaccessible to majority of them. With the help of Dynos, Fiola recognized that lowering prices during off hours would allow it to tap into this nearby market. Doing so would increase sales, albeit at lower margins, but also reduce waste of their highly perishable foods, such as fish.

From the business perspective, at a minimum dynamic pricing increases profits for restaurants, an industry with notoriously tight margins. But Sharda added an interesting twist: he suggested that the additional revenue generated by his dynamic pricing tool could even offset the restaurant's overall costs, thereby making it much more accessible to all. I also like Dynos because it allows people to afford and enjoy items that were previously unattainable. Kind of like the job lot strawberries my grandparents used to sell.

LEAN PATH

Next up on my Top 5 list is *Lean Path*, yet another technology-fueled, food waste prevention startup. *Lean Path* was founded in 2014 on the belief that food waste is one of the world's most pressing challenges, one that harms the environment, contributes to global hunger, and can hurt a business's bottom line. Its mission is as straightforward as it is monumental, and on its own enough to secure a spot on my Top 5 list:

To end avoidable food waste in our world.

Despite the best efforts of organizations and businesses like the NRDC and ReFed, Americans still know very little about their waste. Vaclav Smil, professor emeritus at the University of Manitoba, Canada, who has written many books and articles on the intersection of food, policy, energy and the environment, said the following: "All countries, except Japan, have only approximate, derived, assumed, secondary waste data."

To understand the implications this has for American business as a whole, we must draw upon another expert, this time from the business world. Peter Drucker is credited with two of the most important quotes in business management, the most relevant in this context being: "If you can't measure it, you can't manage it."

Lean Path does just that: it measures. It leverages savvy technology, data science, and a team of cooks to help organizations to understand how and why food is being wasted, then how to take action to achieve measurable results.

Lean Path operates under the conviction that the future of food service depends on the power of technology and data science. As stated on its website, the future of food service "will be won by those that arm their teams with the people-friendly tools they need to maximize productivity and minimize waste. It will be won by innovators that realize, wasted food is a wasted opportunity." Technology such as that of *Lean Path* helps encourage and create good organizational food waste habits (thereby increasing food-telligence).

HIDDEN HARVEST

Fourth on my Top 5 list is Hidden Harvest. According to its website, Hidden Harvest is a produce recovery program, with a twofold mission:

- To employ low-income farm workers at a pay above the prevailing wage; and
- To 'rescue' locally grown produce that is left behind in the fields and orchards after harvest or in packing houses, and use it to feed the poor and hungry.

Since 2001, Hidden Harvest has harvested over 14 million pounds of fresh, surplus crops from the Coachella Valley fields and area packing houses in California. All of the rescued produce is been distributed to nearly 50,000 people every month through the startup's own programs and its partner agencies that serve low-income families. Hidden Harvest made my list because it was one of the first startups to address the growing issue of abandoned food, which I discussed in more detail earlier in the book, and is still one of the few start-ups working in this problem area. I also like the clear focus on social good and the ongoing educational opportunities and events Hidden Harvest sponsors.

And...

MISFIT JUICERY

Last on my list of Top 5 food waste prevention startups is my absolute favorite: Misfit Juicery. Misfit was founded by two good friends and former Georgetown students, Ann Yang and Philip Wong. As the name suggests, Misfit makes juice, but does so with a twist, or twisted fruit to be more precise.

Misfit's mission says it all:

We've made it our mission to stop food waste in its tracks. Our juices are made with "ugly" produce that usually fills landfills because they don't fit our grocery beauty ideals. We love our Misfits, and you will too.

The company was formed in 2015 out of the co-founders' passion for addressing the food waste problem outlined in more detail in the first part of this book. Seventy percent of its juices are made up of misfits: "the oddball produce that farmers can't sell," today's version of job lots, and other left-over scraps like the ones salvaged on the farm near Toulouse. The company's products are being sold in popular stores and food chains all around the country, and it will soon branch out to sell to offices and restaurants. I know this because I have just been hired to launch this part of their venture! (This is another reason Misfit made it to my Top 5 List.) In fact, by employing me, it has also placed me on the path to become the next-generation Food Waste Warrior in my family. So in other words, the legacy continues!

CONCLUSION

———

In case my book didn't tip you off, I am an extroverted person; I love talking to and learning from others. When it came to researching the topic of food waste, this translated into lots of hands-on learning. I attended committees, potlucks and conferences, and I interviewed people in every sector related to this field. I spoke to them over the phone or in person, but I also had a few chance encounters in elevators and even got to interact with a glitch-ridden chat service of a food donation app. I talked to farmers, government officials, restaurant owners, caterers, entrepreneurs, and nonprofit employees, as well as grocery store owners, like those in my family.

One of the last people I reached out to was the self-proclaimed "*Wasted Food Dude,*" Jonathan Bloom. Bloom is one of the leading authorities in the field of food waste, having worked in the field since 2005, and also an award-winning author. His 12 years of experience would, in today's terms, practically be equal to a century in the food waste world. This is due in large part to technology, which is changing rapidly and laying the groundwork that enables many of the most popular food-waste-fighting solutions today. Think of companies like *Lean Path*, showcased above, or even *Olio*, an app that makes donating your food as easy as taking a picture. "When I was writing *American Wasteland*," Bloom said, "my priority number one was to open people's eyes to this problem... The biggest thing that has changed since then is that [the] problem is on more people's radars."

I was happy to hear that food waste has 'moved up the food chain,' so to speak, and is on many people's minds. It certainly was on mine when I returned to Georgetown's campus in the fall of 2017 for my 5th semester.

As at the beginning of previous academic periods, I started with some commitments, school-related 'New Year's resolutions' so to speak. A few in the past have been:

- This semester, I'll get more sleep;
- This semester, I am going to work out more; and
- This semester, I am going to procrastinate less.

At the beginning of my fifth semester, it was all about food waste and I wanted to take it further than just making an oral proclamation. That's when I decided to engage my roommate Joe. Joe had not only heard all of my food waste stories and witnessed my food-saving endeavors, but he was also notoriously fond of legal documents. He would draft elaborate agreements even for the most frivolous of matters. I once even served as a witness on a contract between him and his best friend Jenifer regarding a $15 dollar loan—with interest— so needless to say, I knew just the guy to ask.

Joe immediately pulled out his ceremonial fountain pen and a legal pad and got to work. Before I knew it, he proudly provided me with my very own Food Waste Prevention Oath of Allegiance and read it to me out loud before my signature.

I, Adrian Hertel, do solemnly swear that I will faithfully execute the Office of Food Waste Warrior of Alumni Square #72 and will, to the best of my ability, preserve, protect and defend the food of this apartment.

"Perfect!" I laughed, feeling quite presidential while I signed the paper. I had my very own constitution.

Living it, however, was a different thing altogether. That required changing habits, one small one at a time. Back on campus, I decided to start with composting. My hometown of Princeton, NJ introduced curbside composting while I was still in high school, so I was used to composting being a rather seamless process. Unfortunately, this task became the first real challenge because campus composting was unheard of at Georgetown. It would have been easy to give up, but watching students chuck half-eaten pizzas reminded me both of my unpleasant experience in Naples and the system I had learned from Duhigg. Over time, it became easier and easier to adopt new routines, and eventually I was able to come up with my own list (see Part III).

My research, personal experiences, and interviews not only showed me that I had a role to play in decreasing the problems associated with food waste—as all individuals do—but also that others, ranging from government bodies to corporations, do as well. Encouraging good food waste habits allows you to influence and educate others, so that more people can reap the benefits of reducing the problem of food waste. And on the topic of reaping benefits, there are many to be had, including capitalizing on food waste to create a new business.

CITATIONS

———

INTRODUCTION:

1. Hall, Kevin D., et al. "The Progressive Increase of Food
    Waste in America and Its Environmental Impact." PLOS
    ONE, Public Library of Science, 25 Nov. 2009, www.jour-
    nals.plos.org/plosone/article?id=10.1371%2Fjournal.
    pone.0007940.

2. FAO. "Key Facts on Food Loss and Waste You Should Know!"
    Food and Agriculture Organization of the United Nations,
    www.fao.org/save-food/resources/keyfindings/en/.

3. Senet, Stéphanie. "Denmark Cuts Food Waste
    by 25%." Euractiv.com, Euractiv, 2 Dec. 2016, www.
    euractiv.com/section/agriculture-food/news/
    denmark-cuts-food-waste-by-25/.

CHAPTER 1:

1. Gunders, Dana, and Jonathan Bloom. Wasted: How America Is Losing up to 40 Percent of Its Food from Farm to Fork to Landfill. Natural Resources Defense Council, 2017, www.nrdc.org/sites/default/files/wasted-food-IP.pdf.

2. FAO. "Key Facts on Food Loss and Waste You Should Know!" Food and Agriculture Organization of the United Nations, www.fao.org/save-food/resources/keyfindings/en/.

3. Gustavsson, Jenny. Global Food Losses and Food Waste: Extent, Causes and Prevention. Food and Agriculture Organization of the United Nations (FAO), 2011, www.fao.org/docrep/014/mb060e/mb060e00.pdf.

4. ReFed. A ROADMAP TO REDUCE U.S. FOOD WASTE BY 20 PERCENT. ReFed, www.refed.com/downloads/ReFED_Report_2016.pdf.

5. BIO-Intelligence Service, and Food and Agriculture Organization of the United Nations (FAO). Food Wastage Footprint: Impacts on Natural Resources: Summary Report. FAO, 2013, www.fao.org/docrep/018/i3347e/i3347e.pdf.

6. EPA. "Sustainable Management of Food Basics." EPA, Environmental Protection Agency, 6 July 2017, www.epa.gov/sustainable-management-food/sustainable-management-food-basics.

7. Coleman-Jensen, Alisha, et al. "Household Food Security in the United States in 2016." USDA ERS, www.ers.usda.gov/publications/pub-details/?pubid=84972.

8. Hall, Kevin D., et al. "The Progressive Increase of Food

Waste in America and Its Environmental Impact." PLOS
ONE, Public Library of Science, 25 Nov. 2009, www.jour-
nals.plos.org/plosone/article?id=10.1371%2Fjournal.
pone.0007940.

9. Hoek, Marga. "Food Waste—a Tremendous Economic
Waste." The Huffington Post, TheHuffingtonPost.com, 16
June 2017, www.huffingtonpost.com/entry/food-waste-a-tre-
mendous-economic-waste_us_5943ca03e4b024b7e0df4afb.

CHAPTER 4:

1. Malone, Robert. "World's Worst Waste." Forbes, Forbes
Magazine, 13 July 2012, www.forbes.com/2006/05/23/waste-
worlds-worst-cx_rm_0524waste.html#1e046eea3d79.

CHAPTER 5:

1. McCarthy, Niall. "The U.S. Cities With The Largest Homeless
Populations [Infographic]." Forbes, Forbes Magazine, 1
Dec. 2016, www.forbes.com/sites/niallmccarthy/2016/11/25/
the-u-s-cities-where-the-largest-homeless-pop-infograph-
ic/#238789e14dde.

2. Berezow, Alex. "Which Cities Have the Most
Homeless People?" Which Cities Have the Most
Homeless People? | American Council on Science
and Health, American Council on Science and
Health, 13 Oct. 2016, www.acsh.org/news/2016/10/13/
which-cities-have-most-homeless-people-10300.

3. California Department of Food and Agriculture. "California

Department of Food and Agriculture." CDFA, www.cdfa. ca.gov/statistics/.

4. "2011–17 California Drought." Wikipedia, Wikimedia Foundation, 3 Mar. 2018, www.en.wikipedia.org/ wiki/2011%E2%80%9317_California_drought.

5. Hall, Kevin D., et al. "The Progressive Increase of Food Waste in America and Its Environmental Impact." PLOS ONE, Public Library of Science, 25 Nov. 2009, www.journals.plos.org/plosone/article?id=10.1371%2Fjournal. pone.0007940.

Printed in Great Britain
by Amazon